READ TO ME! TEACH ME!

For my parents who began my love
for children's books with bedtime stories,
my sisters who shared them,
and
my husband who often listens to them
over dinner.

READ TO ME! TEACH ME!

by Mary Jane Mangini Rossi

Cover photograph by Barbara Campbell
Design by One Plus One Studio, New York City
ISBN 0-940212-07-2
Printed and bound in the United States of America
Published by American Baby Books
Wauwatosa, WI 53226
Published simultaneously in Canada

CONTENTS

INTRODUCTION

I love children, and I love books. It's no surprise then that I love children's books. Thanks to my parents this love affair began when I was a child. Luckily, I have never outgrown it. In fact, my love for children's books has deepened especially since I am now able to enthusiastically share it with others. Like Owliver the owl, I have found my special place in the world—as a college instructor of children's literature, as an early childhood educator, as a children's book reviewer, and as creator of The Book Stork, a mail-order children's book consultation and selection service.

Many people like to curl up with a good book and a cup of tea. I like to curl up with a good book and a child. Fortunately, my work allows me this pleasure. With my wide-eyed and open-eared young listeners, I have befriended not-so-scary Wild Things and closet-dwelling nightmares and have grieved over the deaths of a spider named Charlotte and a cat named Barney. I have travelled to Paris with Madeleine and under a dining room table with Frances the badger. I have cheered a Little Engine that proved she could and loved a teddy bear even though his overalls were missing a button. I have enjoyed all the wonders of a snowy day with Peter and have narrowly escaped from a vegetable garden with another Peter. I have laughed and cried, applauded and empathized, smiled in delight, and trembled in anticipation all through the pages of children's books.

I invite you to share the same adventures with your child—to begin his or her love affair with books and perhaps, to become enamored of them yourself. This book is my cordial invitation to you to take your child's hand and tumble down a rabbit hole, fly to Never-never-land, travel to the House at Pooh Corner and to the Little House on the Prairie, set sail with Max "through night and day and in and out of weeks" and over the years to the land of children's books.

On this journey you will see many sites of interest. This tour is intended to make you feel comfortable in the world of children's books, to make you love it and, of course, return to it over and over again. This book is a comprehensive, convenient guide to help you wisely select appropriate books for your child from birth through age five. Studies have proven that children who are introduced to books as babies and who are read to frequently and encouraged to think and talk about the pictures, characters, and situations they meet in books become good readers. They learn to read because they have a positive attitude toward reading and books. They see books as an adventure to be explored, as treasure to be discovered.

Like most parents, you probably realize the importance of books in the development of your child but are overwhelmed by the large quantity *and* quality of children's books available today. With over 40,000 children's books in print and 3,000 new titles published each year, your dilemma is an understandable one. Even if your intentions are good, your selection should not be random. You should be prepared with a definite set of evaluative criteria; you should know which types of books are suitable for your child at different developmental levels.

This book is intended to make your selection easier. In each chapter I discuss types of books that are appropriate at particular ages. Of course, since all children develop at varying rates and have different personal preferences, my age groupings are general. And there is a great deal of overlapping. For instance, the poetry discussed in Chapter 6 and the songbooks and Mother Goose rhymes discussed in Chapter 1 are suitable for all ages. For easy reference, I have ended each chapter with a select, author-alphabetized, thematically-arranged list of books, and at the end of the book, I have included a bibliography of adult books about children's literature and child development for further reading. I have read all of the children's books recommended and have used most of them successfully with children. All of them are nonsexist and of outstanding literary and artistic merit. Many are my favorites and favorites of my students—the four-year-olds and the sixty-four-year-olds. Hopefully, some will become your child's favorites—and yours, for I have written this book for your child *and* for the child in you. So come with me to the land of children's books.

CHAPTER 1
AGES BIRTH TO ONE

*A mother once asked a clergyman when she should begin the education of
her child, who she told him was then four years old. "Madam," was the reply,
"you have lost three years already. From the very first smile that gleams
over an infant's cheek, your opportunity begins."*
—*Whatley*

The time to introduce your child to the magic and wonder of books is not a few weeks before he begins first grade or even nursery school, but now—when he is still in the cradle. Children's literature specialists Dorothy Butler, author of *Babies Need Books*, and Nancy Larrick, author of *A Parent's Guide to Children's Reading*, agree, emphasizing that 50 percent of intellectual development takes place between birth and four years of age, another 30 percent before the age of eight.

Many people mistakenly view infants as passive bundles of joy, incapable of any real learning. The fairly recent research of Swiss psychologist Jean Piaget and others has established that infants are indeed active initiators of behavior, quite capable of absorbing and learning. Consequently, they should be encouraged by their parents, their first teachers, to respond to and interact with stimuli in their environment—people, toys, mobiles, paintings, music, and books. Books offer infants much-needed visual and aural stimulation. Through appropriate picturebooks your baby will learn to focus on illustrations and will babble in response to soothing, rhythmic texts. And sharing books with your infant will give you a quiet, peaceful time that can only heighten the bonding experience.

SIMPLE BOOKS

Infants are attracted to books with bright, simple, boldly defined illustrations. Dick Bruna's are among the best books designed for the very young child. Each book in his popular series, which includes *The Apple, Circus,* and *Miffy*, features simple, primary-colored pictures. Margaret Borrett's *Baby's First Book* is also suitable. Highlighted by realistic, colorful pictures, this book also includes a lower-case label for each object for later use. Other illustrators whose styles are appropriate for infants are Celestino Piatti, whose Rouaultlike pictures are boldly outlined in black; Jan Pienkowski, whose tiny books resemble Bruna's; and Brian Wildsmith, who favors geometric shapes and carnival colors. Many books mentioned throughout this book such as the Teddy Board Books and the Price/ Stern/Sloan board books are also appropriate to use with your infant.

SONGBOOKS

Your baby's nursery will not be complete without a selection of songbooks. Their melodies will be hummed, whispered, whistled, shouted, and loved throughout childhood and maybe even beyond. An especially appealing songbook for infants because of its large format and brightly colored, full-page pictures is *Sleep, Baby, Sleep*, Trudi Oberhänsli's beautifully illustrated version of a well-known and well-loved German lullaby. Other noteworthy titles include *Lullabies and Nightsongs*, a collection of new and rearranged traditional cradle songs illustrated by Maurice Sendak; Elizabeth Poston's *The Baby's Song Book*, an anthology of traditional nursery songs accompanied by piano arrangements; Walter Crane's *The Baby's Opera: A Book of Old Rhymes With New Dresses*, a collection of familiar nursery rhymes such as "Lavender's Blue," "Mulberry Bush," and "Jack and Jill" set to music; and Joseph Moorat's *Nursery Rhymes*, the Metropolitan Museum of Art's collection of Mother Goose songs, including "Looby Loo," "Three Blind Mice," and "The Fox Went Out on a Chilly Night," enhanced by Paul Woodroffe's watercolors, a hand-lettered text, and musical notations.

MOTHER GOOSE BOOKS

Mother Goose is ideal for infants. The youngest child will readily respond to the brightly colored pictorial interpretations of these age-old verses and to the rich aural stimulation they generously offer. Babies who are just beginning to become familiar with the modulating sounds and nuances of language delight in nursery rhymes' gentle, melodic language patterns—for instance, the rhythm of "Three Men in a Tub" and "Little Bo Peep" and the alliteration of "Hey Diddle Diddle" and "Baa, Baa Black Sheep." British Educational Psychologist Nicholas Tucker emphasizes that "nursery rhymes with their easily memorized rhymes, alliterative titles, and infectious foot-tapping rhythms are ideally formed to help a baby master speech." Some rhymes become familiar because they purposely leave a space for the baby's own name ("And there will be plenty for _____ and me!"), and others invite a verbal response by a question and answer technique.

An exceptionally good first Mother Goose book is Kay Chorao's *The Baby's Lap Book*, a wonderful collection of nursery rhymes most often sung to infants like "Rock-a-bye Baby," "This Little Pig Went to Market," "Twinkle Twinkle Little Star," and "Pat-a-Cake." Intentionally designed to be read with book and baby cradled on your lap, Chorao has filled her humorous pictures with playful children and cuddly animals. In fact, she has actually transformed some characters into animals; her Old King Cole is a merry brown bear and her astonished pie-loving king in "Sing a Song of Sixpence" is a pudgy pig!

Other appropriate Mother Goose anthologies include *The Real Mother Goose*, a large-sized book familiar for its distinctive black and white checkered border and complemented by Blanche Fisher Wright's colorful, nostalgic illustrations; *Marguerite de Angeli's Book of Nursery and Mother Goose Rhymes*, another large-sized volume of rhymes enhanced by old-fashioned illustrations in a picturesque English setting; and *Brian Wildsmith's Mother Goose*, a more limited selection of rhymes that is beautifully highlighted by bright, kaleidoscopic watercolors in a medieval setting.

From *The Baby's Lap Book* by Kay Chorao. Copyright © 1977 by Kay Sproat Chorao. Reprinted by permission of the publisher, E.P. Dutton.

As your baby grows, Mother Goose will grow along with him. This wonderful old woman will happily accompany your child throughout infancy and into each stage of development. As your infant enters toddlerhood, she will join in the rhymes, not only verbally but physically as well. "Ring a Ring o' Roses," "London Bridge," "One, Two, Buckle My Shoe," and many other verses encourage active participation. Although he will still be delighted by the sound of words, your toddler will listen to the stories these rhythmic words tell, especially since they deal with things that interest young children such as animals ("Mary Had a Little Lamb"), weather ("Rain, Rain, Go Away"), and common occurrences like losing mittens ("Three Little Kittens"). And since the majority of the rhymes are short and action-filled (Jack *jumps* over the candlestick, the cow *jumps* over the moon), they will be well suited to your toddler's still-short attention span. As a preschooler your child will discover new delights like the many riddles, tongue-twisters, and puzzles. And, as Nicholas Tucker points out, as your child enjoys these rhymes, his linguistic development will be furthered by their "comparatively complex grammatical structures" and wide vocabulary. My preschoolers especially like the humor of Mother Goose; they respond with laughter to both nonsense ("And the dish ran away with the spoon.") and misfortune ("Jack fell down and broke his crown."). They also enjoy illustrating the rhymes (after all, who can resist drawing a big, round Humpty Dumpty?), creating their own verses, and pantomiming the action that abounds in Mother Goose land.

Since Mother Goose will be your child's lifelong companion, choose carefully from the wide assortment of nursery rhyme books available today. Examine the book's format. Do you prefer a large-sized volume like Blanche Fisher Wright's or a small, child-sized book like Kate Greenaway's? Is the paper quality good? Are the endpapers plain, or are they decorated with a motif from the book's illustrations? Is an index included? a title index? an index of first lines? Examine the content. How many rhymes are included? (Remember there are

From Celestino Piatti, *The Happy Owls.* Copyright © 1963 by Artemis Verlags-Aktiengesellshaft. (New York: Atheneum, 1964.) Reprinted with the permission of Atheneum Publishers.

Illustration Dick Bruna, copyright © Mercis b.v., 1972.

over 1,000.) Which ones are included? Are they popular or obscure ones? Examine the illustrations. Are they spaced properly with the text? Is their setting modern like Briggs' or nostalgic like de Angeli's? Is it urban or rural? What is their style? (Beware! Many illustrators' interpretations of Mother Goose are overly sentimental, others are simply literal and boring. The very best are imaginative, clever, and perceptive, adding their own magic while enhancing the magic of Mother Goose's words, which are, as Andrew Lang described them, "smooth stones from the brook of time, worn round by constant friction of tongues long silent.") Ask yourself: Do the illustrations truly complement the text? Do they interpret it or merely decorate it? Do they convey the mood of the rhymes? Do you prefer the soft pencil drawings of Chorao or the bright watercolors of Wildsmith?

Baby books, songbooks, and Mother Goose books will be carried into your baby's first year along with favorite teddy bears and blankets. But there are many more treasures awaiting your one-year-old.

BOOKS FOR INFANTS

These books are appropriate to use with your infant, and many will probably become favorites to be read over and over again as your child grows. For easy reference, they are grouped thematically and alphabetized by author. Those mentioned in this chapter are marked with an asterisk (*).

Baby Books
*Borrett, Margaret. *Baby's First Book.* Ladybird.
*Bruna, Dick. *The Apple, Circus, The Egg, The Fish, The King, Lisa and Lynn, The Little*

Bird, the Miffy series, *The Sailor, The School, Snuffy, Snuffy and the Fire* plus other Bruna titles mentioned in upcoming chapters. Methuen.

*Pienkowski, Jan. *Weather.* Harvey House, 1980 plus other titles mentioned in next chapter.

*Piatti, Celestino. *The Happy Owls.* Atheneum, 1964.

Songbooks

Aliki. *Hush Little Baby: A Folk Lullaby.* Prentice-Hall, 1968.

*Crane, Walter, ill. *The Baby's Opera: A Book of Old Rhymes With New Dresses.* Windmill/Simon & Schuster, 1981.

*Engvick, William, ed. *Lullabies and Nightsongs.* Maurice Sendak, ill. Harper, 1965.

*Moorat, Joseph, arranger. *Nursery Songs.* Paul Woodroffe, ill. The Metropolitan Museum of Art and Thames and Hudson, 1980.

*Oberhänsli, Trudi, ill. *Sleep, Baby, Sleep.* Atheneum, 1967, out of print.

Opie, Iona and Peter. *A Nursery Companion.* Oxford University Press, 1981.

*Poston, Elizabeth, compiler. *The Baby's Song Book.* William Stobbs, ill. Crowell, 1972.

Swados, Elizabeth. *Lullaby.* Faith Hubley, ill. Harper, 1980.

Zemach, Margot, ill. *Hush, Little Baby.* Dutton, 1976.

Mother Goose Books

Bayley, Nicola, ill. *Nicola Bayley's Book of Nursery Rhymes.* Knopf, 1977.

*Briggs, Raymond, ill. *The Mother Goose Treasury.* Coward, 1966.

Brooks, Leslie, ill. *Ring O'Roses: A Nursery Rhyme Picture Book.* new ed., Warne, 1977.

Caldecott, Randolph, ill. *Hey Diddle Diddle Picture Book.* Warne.

*Chorao, Kay, ill. *The Baby's Lap Book.* Dutton, 1977.

*de Angeli, Marguerite, ill. *Marguerite de Angeli's Book of Nursery and Mother Goose Rhymes.* Doubleday, 1954.

*Greenaway, Kate, ill. *Mother Goose or The Old Nursery Rhymes.* Warne, 1882.

Jeffers, Susan, ill. *If Wishes Were Horses: Mother Goose Rhymes.* Dutton, 1979.

———*Three Jovial Huntsmen: A Mother Goose Rhyme.* Bradbury, 1973.

Ness, Evaline, ill. *Old Mother Hubbard and Her Dog.* Holt, 1972.

Opie, Iona and Peter, ill. *The Puffin Book of Nursery Rhymes.* Penguin, 1964.

Rackham, Arthur, ill. *Mother Goose.* Viking, 1975.

Reed, Philip, ill. *Mother Goose and Nursery Rhymes.* Atheneum, 1963.

Rojankovsky, Feodor, ill. *The Tall Book of Mother Goose.* Harper, 1942.

Sendak, Maurice, ill. *Hector Protector and As I Went Over the Water.* Harper, 1965.

Spier, Peter, ill. *London Bridge Is Falling Down!* Doubleday, 1967.

Tarrant, Margaret, ill. *Nursery Rhymes.* Crowell, 1978.

Tudor, Tasha, ill. *Mother Goose.* Walck, 1944.

*Wildsmith, Brian, ill. *Brian Wildsmith's Mother Goose.* Watts, 1964.

*Wright, Blanche Fisher, ill. *The Real Mother Goose.* Rand McNally, 1916.

CHAPTER 2
AGES ONE TO TWO

Childhood is like a mirror, which reflects in after life the images first presented to it.
—Samuel Smiles

As a one-year-old your baby will hum and sing, imitate sounds and words, point to body parts when asked, and take off shoes and socks when not asked. One-year-olds love to be entertained; they also like *to* entertain dolls, stuffed animals, and other special friends with picturebooks. By now your baby can probably recognize, point to, and name familiar objects in pictures. Although his attention span is very short, your one-year-old will enjoy simple stories with repetitive words and phrases and will soon be thrilled to supply the last word of a line for you. As language acquisition increases so does small muscle coordination. Your child will now enthusiastically reach for, grasp, and attempt to turn the pages of a book, an accomplishment that makes durable books a necessity. Eating books is also a common feat at this age. When Francis Bacon said, "Some books are to be tasted, others to be swallowed, and some few to be chewed and digested," he didn't intend to be taken literally, but your one-year-old will do just that. Don't despair! An attempt at eating books simply means that books interest your child and that she is trying to get to know them better. Encourage this relationship with song and fingerplay books, board books, name-the-object books, bedtime stories, and simple concept books.

SONGBOOKS AND FINGERPLAY BOOKS

Since one-year-olds love to be sung to, now is the time to explore more songbooks, especially since your child will now be joining in on some of the lyrics. Noteworthy titles include *The Fireside Book of Children's Songs* with over 100 selections; *The Fireside Book of Folk Songs* with traditional ballads, work songs, holiday carols, and marching tunes accompanied by both piano arrangements and guitar chords; and *Mister Rogers' Songbook*, which includes the well-loved "You Are Special" and "Won't You Be My Neighbor?"

Songbooks that include fingerplays are especially suitable now that your child will enjoy mimicking your hand movements. Good choices are Marc Brown's *Finger Rhymes*, which includes favorites like "Eensy Weensy Spider," "Where Is Thumbkin?" and "There Was a Little Turtle"; Tom Glazer's *Eye Winker, Tom Tinker, Chin Chopper* and its companion vol-

15

ume *Do Your Ears Hang Low? Fifty More Musical Fingerplays;* and *Wee Sing,* a collection of 70 songs and fingerplays created by two music teachers.

BOARD BOOKS AND NAME-THE-OBJECT BOOKS

Your one-year-old is now ready for sturdy board books. Although cloth books are making a comeback, I recommend board books because cloth books are generally of a much lower artistic and literary merit and their life span is much briefer than that of the durable, plastic-coated, washable board books. Luckily, publishers are finally realizing the importance of books for babies and are producing more quality board books than ever.

Noteworthy examples are Random House's rounded-corner board books that include Harry McNaught's *Trucks,* Eloise Wilkins' *Nursery Rhymes,* and Tony Chen's *Wild Animals;* Grosset & Dunlap's Gyo Fujikawa-illustrated board books that feature multiracial characters and Teddy Board Books with bright color photographs; Simon & Schuster's Helen Oxenbury series; and Dial's Max series by Rosemary Wells. Other favorites are Robert Kraus' abridged versions of *Leo the Late Bloomer* and *Milton the Early Riser,* his *Animal Families,* and his glow-in-the-dark bedtime book *See the Moon.*

Because of their uncluttered pictures and simple formats, most board books make excellent name-the-object books. Your observant one-year-old will enjoy naming and having you name familiar objects in picturebooks. These "pictures should be clear and natural," emphasize Laurie and Joseph Braga in their book *Learning and Growing,* "depicting objects within [your] child's experience so he begins to recognize pictorial and two-dimensional representations of the objects that he knows in three-dimensions. This is the beginning of recognition of symbolic representation that he will have to acquire in later learning of reading, writing, and arithmetic." Along with board books other simply illustrated picturebooks will serve as good "name-the-object" books. Suitable ones include Margaret Wise Brown's *The Big Red Barn,* whose rhyming text introduces farm animals; Satomi Ichikawa's *Let's Play,* which encourages young children to recognize and name familiar playthings; and Dick Bruna's popular books. Golden Touch and Feel Books with small formats, sturdy pages, spiral bindings, and textured illustrations are also excellent. Favorites in this series include Dorothy Kunhardt's *Pat the Bunny* and Eve and Pat Witte's *The Touch Me Book.*

BEDTIME STORIES

Bedtime books (which aren't just for bedtime!) are plentiful, ranging from simple animal goodnight books to longer sleepy-time stories, from anthologies of nighttime poems to people goodnight books. One of the most popular is Margaret Wise Brown's classic *Good-*

From *Goodnight, Goodnight* by Eve Rice. Copyright © 1980 by Eve Rice. Reprinted with permission of Greenwillow Books, a division of William Morrow & Company, Inc.

night Moon. "Goodnight bears/Goodnight chairs/Goodnight kittens/And Goodnight mittens." A little rabbit says goodnight to all the things in her room, and, as she does, the gentle rhyming text and successive darkening of the pictures lull young listeners (and maybe even some parents) to sleep. A more recent yet equally effective bedtime book is Eve Rice's *Goodnight, Goodnight.* "Goodnight came over the rooftops slowly," begins this simple story that follows the goodnight rituals of townspeople (for instance, a grocer rolls up his awning, a man says goodnight to his parrot, a mama says goodnight to her baby) till "Goodnight settled softly on the buildings all around." Rice's striking black and white cityscapes highlighted with touches of bright yellow for the full moon glowingly complement her soothing text. Karla Kuskin's *Night Again,* which gently traces bedtime rituals from climbing the stairs to prayers to saying goodnight to favorite stuffed bears, is also comforting as is Russell Hoban's *Bedtime for Frances,* in which a procrastinating little badger cleverly tries to postpone bedtime. Sylvia Plath's *The Bed Book* is a whimsical poem about all kinds of beds —submarine beds, snack-bar beds, jet-propelled beds, "not just a white little/tucked-in tight little/nighty-night little/turn-out-the-light little bed!"

> "Keep a poem in your pocket
> And a picture in your head
> And you'll never feel lonely
> At night when you're in bed."

Your child will be comforted by this Beatrice Schenk de Regniers' poem and other traditional and contemporary poems such as the anonymously written "Now I Lay Me Down to

Sleep," Gwendolyn Brooks' "Pete at the Zoo," and Leland Jacobs' "How Far?" in *Go to Bed! A Book of Bedtime Poems* edited by Lee Bennett Hopkins. Another excellent collection of nighttime poems is Susan Russo's *The Moon's the North Wind's Cookie*, which features poems by well-known writers including Vachel Lindsay, Robert Louis Stevenson, Karla Kuskin, Nikki Giovanni, Joan Aiken, and Myra Cohen Livingston.

CONCEPT BOOKS

Since your one-year-old's attention span is limited, now is a good time for simple alphabet and counting books. The number of concept books is overwhelming; it seems that each season publishing houses produce several new ones. Some are trite and uninspiring; others are innovative, imaginative, and truly captivating. Since a good concept book should actually be able to grow with your child, it's essential that you choose concept books carefully. Be critical when evaluating ABC, counting, and other concept books, and ask yourself the following questions: Do the text and pictures correspond? Are only one or two objects per page represented? (Remember, cluttered, busy pictures generally confuse young children.) Are the illustrations clearly defined and easily identifiable? Are letters and numbers clear? Are both upper-case and lower-case letters shown? Are confusing letter sounds like "K is for knife" avoided? Are objects that are known by more than one name avoided? (B is for bunny—or is it a rabbit?)

Unfortunately, even some of the very best concept books are occasionally not without fault. For example, Dick Bruna includes only lower-case letters and chooses a toadstool to represent "T" and a rabbit to represent "B" in *B Is for Bear* (also available as *ABC Frieze*). Luckily, with a little ingenuity you can solve these minor problems. I paste construction paper capital letters on my *ABC Frieze*, which stretches across my classroom wall, and explain to my young students that many things have more than one name—like mushroom and toadstool and bunny and rabbit. Despite these flaws Dick Bruna's books, including *I Can Count*, *I Can Dress Myself*, and *Dick Bruna's Animal Book*, are among the very best designed for young children. Their small format is perfect for little hands, and their simple texts and uncluttered, primary-colored pictures make them ideal for your one-year-old. Louise Bates Ames, associate director of the Gesell Institute of Child Development, calls Bruna's books "superb—the most enchanting that I know of for the very young...books not only to look at and listen to, but also to carry around and love." And, like the very best concept books, they will be loved as your child grows older since Bruna books are quite at home in both the crib and the kindergarten classroom.

Jan Pienkowski's Brunalike books that include *Colors*, *Shapes*, and *Numbers* are also suitable now as is Eric Carle's *My Very First Book of Numbers*. This split-book, or "broken book" as one toddler described it to me, encourages children to match a picture on the bottom half of the page with a numeral on the top half. Its durable board pages and spiral binding are practical, making flipping pages easier for small fingers. Besides these tiny books, also introduce your child to colorful, large-format concept books like *Brian Wildsmith's 1,2,3's*, whose kaleidoscopic pictures of various geometric shapes illustrate the numbers one to ten, and Eric Carle's *1,2,3 to the Zoo*, in which a trainful of animals ride to their new home—a zoo. Carle includes the numerals at the upper left-hand corner of each double-page spread, and, as a story-building and page-turning incentive for older pre-readers, a miniature train travels across the bottom of the pages and a little mouse "hides" in each picture. Another noteworthy counting book is Tana Hoban's *Count and See*, a collection of striking black and white photographs of familiar objects accompanied by numbers shown as words and numerals.

Another large-format book that is appropriate now is *Brian Wildsmith's ABC*. Ablaze with color this book features familiar objects such as a butterfly, an elephant, and a copper tea kettle and some not-so-familiar objects such as a unicorn, a windmill, and an iguana. Also suitable is C. B. Falls' 1923 classic *ABC Book*, which is famous for its distinctive woodcuts, and Wanda Gag's *The ABC Bunny*, an action-packed rhyming storybook highlighted by capital letters reminiscent of wooden blocks.

More concept books await your child as his or her second birthday approaches along with simple storybooks, wordless books, and response books.

BOOKS FOR ONE-YEAR-OLDS

Use this list together with the list in Chapter 1 and the list at the end of Chapter 3. For easy reference, books are grouped thematically and author-alphabetized. Those mentioned within this chapter are marked with an asterisk (*).

*Beall, Pamela Conn and Susan Hagan Nipp. *Wee Sing*. Price/Stern/Sloan.

*Boni, Margaret and Norman Lloyd, compilers. *The Fireside Book of Folk Songs*. Alice and Martin Provenson, ill. Simon & Schuster, 1967.

*Brown, Marc, compiler and illustrator. *Finger Rhymes*. Dutton, 1980.

*Glazer, Tom. *Eye Winker, Tom Tinker, Chin Chopper*. Ron Himler, ill. Doubleday, 1973.

*———*Do Your Ears Hang Low? Fifty More Musical Fingerplays*. Doubleday, 1975.

Larrick, Nancy, compiler. *The Wheels on the Bus Go Round and Round, School Bus Songs and Chants*. Gene Holtan, ill. Children's Press, 1972.

*Rogers, Fred. *Mr. Rogers' Songbook*. Steven Kellogg, ill. Random House, 1970.

Seeger, Ruth, ed. *American Folk Songs for Children*. Barbara Cooney, ill. Doubleday, 1953.

Spier, Peter, ill. *The Fox Went Out on a Chilly Night*. Doubleday, 1961.

———*London Bridge Is Falling Down*. Doubleday, 1967.

*Winn, Marie, ed. *The Fireside Book of Children's Songs*. John Alcorn, ill. Simon & Schuster, 1966.

Board Books and Name-the-Object Books

Bonforte, Lisa. *Farm Animals*. Random House, 1981.

*Brown, Margaret Wise. *The Big Red Barn*. Rosella Hartman, ill. Addison-Wesley, 1965.

*Chen, Tony. *Wild Animals*. Random House, 1981.

*Fujikawa, Gyo. *Let's Eat*. Grosset & Dunlap, 1975.

———— *My Favorite Things.* Grosset & Dunlap, 1978.

———— *Puppies, Pussy Cats and Other Friends.* Grosset & Dunlap, 1975.

———— *Sleepytime.* Grosset & Dunlap, 1975.

*Ichikawa, Satomi. *Let's Play.* Philomel, 1981.

*Kraus, Robert. *Animal Families.* Jose Aruego and Ariane Dewey, ill. Windmill/Simon & Schuster, 1980.

*———— *Leo the Late Bloomer.* (abridged). Windmill/Simon & Schuster, 1971.

*———— *Milton the Early Riser.* (abridged). Windmill/Simon & Schuster, 1972.

———— *Mouse Work.* (from *Another Mouse to Feed*). Windmill/Simon & Schuster, 1980.

*———— *See the Moon.* Windmill/Simon & Schuster, 1980.

*Kunhardt, Dorothy. *Pat the Bunny.* (A Touch and Feel Book). Western Press, 1962. Other Touch and Feel Books include Eve and Pat Witte's *The Touch Me Book,* 1961; *Who Lives There?* 1961; and *The Telephone Book,* 1975.

McNaught, Harry. *Animal Babies.* Random House, 1976.

*———— *Trucks.* Random House, 1976.

Miller, J. P. *Big and Little.* Random House, 1977.

*Oxenbury, Helen. *Dressing, Family, Friends, Playing, Working.* Simon & Schuster, 1981.

Pfloog, Jan. *Kittens.* Random House, 1977.

———— *Puppies.* Random House, 1979.

Roosevelt, Michele Chopin. *Animals in the Woods.* Random House, 1981.

*Wells, Rosemary. *Max's First Word, Max's New Suit, Max's Ride, Max's Toys: A Counting Book.* Dial, 1979.

*Wilkins, Eloise. *Nursery Rhymes.* Random House, 1979.

Wynne, Patricia. *Animal ABC.* Random House, 1977.

*Teddy Board Books including *Baby's First Counting Book, Baby's First Toys, Baby's First Book, Baby's First ABC.* Platt & Munk.

At the Table, Looking at Animals, In the House, Going for a Ride. Price/Stern/Sloan (Holland), 1979.

Bedtime Books

Brown, Margaret Wise. *A Child's Goodnight Book,* Jean Chalot, ill. Harper, 1943.

*———— *Goodnight Moon.* Clement Hurd, ill. Harper, 1947.

———— *Little Fur Family.* Garth Williams, ill. Harper, 1968.

Hazen, Barbara Shook. *Where Do Bears Sleep?* Ian E. Staunton, ill. Addison-Wesley, 1970.

*Hoban, Russell. *Bedtime for Frances.* Garth Williams, ill. Harper, 1960.

*Hopkins, Lee Bennett, ed. *Go to Bed! A Book of Bedtime Poems.* Rosekrans Hoffman, ill. Knopf, 1979.

Hutchins, Pat. *Goodnight, Owl!* Macmillan, 1972.

Jacobs, Leland. *Goodnight, Mr. Beetle.* Holt, 1971.

*Kuskin, Karla. *Night Again.* Little Brown, 1981.

Marzollo, Jean. *Close Your Eyes.* Susan Jeffers, ill. Dial, 1978.

Peterson, Jean Whitehouse. *While the Moon Shines Bright.* Margot Apple, ill. Harper, 1981.

*Plath, Sylvia. *The Bed Book.* Emily Arnold McCully, ill. Harper, 1976.

*Rice, Eve. *Goodnight, Goodnight.* Greenwillow, 1980.

*Russo, Susan, compiler and illustrator. *The Moon's the North Wind's Cookie.* Lothrop, 1979.

Schneider, Nina. *While Susie Sleeps.* Dagmar Wilson, ill. Addison-Wesley, 1948.

Stoddard, Sandol. *Bedtime Mouse.* Lynn Munsinger, ill. Houghton Mifflin, 1981.

Watson, Slyde. *Midnight Moon.* Susanna Natti, ill. Philomel, 1979.

Zolotow, Charlotte. *Flocks of Birds.* Ruth Bornstein, ill. Crowell, 1981.

—— *The Sleepy Book.* Vladimir Bobri, ill. Lothrop, 1958.

Concept Books
ABC Books

*Bruna, Dick. *B Is for Bear.* (also available as *ABC Frieze*). Methuen, 1977.

Crane, Walter. *Baby's Own Alphabet.* Dodd, out of print.

*Falls, C. B. *ABC Book.* Doubleday, 1923.

*Gag, Wanda. *The ABC Bunny.* Coward, 1933.

Matthiesen, Thomas. *ABC: An Alphabet Book.* Platt & Munk, 1968.

Munari, Bruno. *Bruno Munari's ABC.* Philomel, 1960.

Tudor, Tasha. *A Is for Annabelle.* Walck, 1954.

*Wildsmith, Brian. *Brian Wildsmith's ABC.* Watts, 1963.

Number Books

*Bruna, Dick. *I Can Count.* (also available as *1,2,3 Frieze*). Methuen, 1968.

*Carle, Eric. *1,2,3 to the Zoo.* Philomel, 1968.

*—— *My Very First Book of Numbers.* Crowell, 1974.

*Hoban, Tana. *Count and See.* Macmillan, 1972.

Peek, Merle. *Roll Over! A Counting Song.* Houghton Mifflin, 1981.

*Pienkowski, Jan. *Colors.* Simon & Schuster, 1981.

*—— *Numbers.* Simon & Schuster, 1981.

*—— *Shapes.* Simon & Schuster, 1981.

—— *ABC.* Simon & Schuster, 1981.

*Wildsmith, Brian. *Brian Wildsmith's 1,2,3's.* Watts, 1965.

CHAPTER 3
AGES TWO TO THREE

*What art can paint or gild any object in after life with the glow which nature gives
to the first baubles of childhood. St. Peter's cannot have the magical power over us that the
red and gold covers of our first picturebook possessed.*
—Ralph Waldo Emerson

Not quite a baby any longer, your two-year-old is now struggling to emerge as an independent person. He probably loves to repeat actions and words over and over again, can confidently kick a ball, and string beads. Your two-year-old also strings words together to form short sentences, readily identifies simple pictures in books, relates pictures to the spoken word, turns pages, and follows sequential events to some extent. Although your child will still enjoy many of the books that she enjoyed throughout babyhood, now is an ideal time to introduce your child to short storybooks with simple plots, wordless picturebooks, participation or response books, and more concept books.

SIMPLE STORYBOOKS

Two-year-olds are generally infatuated with themselves. They are content playing alone. They delight themselves. They amuse themselves. They are, in a word, egocentric. Since two-year-olds have short attention spans and are interested in things that pertain solely to themselves and their immediate environment, their books should be brief and reflect this interest.

Several books by Marie Hall Ets fill these requirements. One of my students' favorites, *Play With Me*, is a simple, rhythmic story of a curious little girl who wanders off into a meadow to play with the shy animals who live there. The book's delicate and softly colored drawings will teach your child to identify a frog, a turtle, a chipmunk, a blue jay, and other woodland creatures. Animals are also introduced in *Just Me*, in which an energetic little boy imitates a series of barnyard animals—climbing like a squirrel, hopping like a rabbit, leaping like a frog, and finally running "like nobody else at all" to greet his father. Other Ets' books loved for their perception, sensitivity, and simplicity are *Gilberto and the Wind* and *In the Forest*.

Ezra Jack Keats' *The Snowy Day* will delight any child who has ever played in the snow and will tantalize those who haven't. Colorful collage illustrations complement a simple text that follows the adventures of little Peter as he slides down a snow mountain, makes tracks in the snow with a stick, waves his arms to make angels in the snow, and explores other wonders of a snowy day—including trying to save a snowball in his jacket pocket!

Eve Rice's *Oh Lewis!* is the very similar saga of a child who is all bundled up yet somehow manages to become all unzippered, unbuttoned, unmittened, unscarfed, and unbooted as he walks along with his mother and sister.

An especially suitable book for temperamental two-year-olds is Edna Mitchell Preston's popular *The Temper Tantrum Book,* which shows young animals stomping, frowning, howling, and generally expressing their anger at various situations that annoy them (and probably your child too) like getting tangles out of hair and getting soap in their eyes. Children love to chime in on the refrain, "I hate it!"

WORDLESS BOOKS

Wordless picturebooks are ideal for two-year-olds, who are learning to master and experiment with language. By inviting children to create their own stories, wordless books encourage verbalization, develop vocabulary, and promote creativity and self-esteem. Although its pictures are nice to look at, a wordless book does not really come alive until a child gives it words and a story. And its story magically changes with each child and with each "re-reading." In this very special way, wordless books become personal. When choosing this type of book for your child, make certain that the illustrations are clear and that the sequence of events is accurate, so your child will be able to follow and interpret the

story easily and develop the habit of following a left to right progression, an essential reading readiness skill.

One of the most ingenious and well-loved wordless books is Pat Hutchins' *Changes, Changes.* Bright, bold drawings show a wooden doll couple cleverly rebuilding their fire-stricken building-block house into—what else?—a fire truck. When a series of mishaps follows, this undaunted couple proves their resourcefulness as they transform their blocks into a boat, a truck, a train, and, finally, back into their very own house. *Changes, Changes* is especially appropriate for young children since building blocks are so familiar to them.

Mercer Mayer's *Ah-Choo* is also popular. Its small format and droll pen and ink pictures make this hilarious tale of the havoc caused by an allergic elephant's sneeze as popular as Mayer's other wordless books: *Hiccup, Oops,* and *Bubble, Bubble.*

Brinton Turkle's *Deep in the Forest,* the wordless adventure of an inquisitive bear cub who fearlessly explores a deserted mountain cabin, is always a winner. Children who are familiar with the story of Goldilocks especially love this reversal story.

RESPONSE BOOKS

Without a doubt two-year-olds love to be read to; they love to be soothed by quiet words, excited by dramatic words, and humored by silly words. But since two-year-olds like to interact with things in their environment, they also like to interact with their books. Not content with merely being observers of the action, two-year-olds like to be participants. They especially like to interpret pictures, look for hidden objects, solve guessing games, answer questions that are directed to them, and join in on repeated words and phrases.

Among the most popular of these participation or response-books are Margaret Wise Brown's Noisy Books, which invite children to help Muffin, a dog, identify various sounds—city sounds, country sounds, winter sounds, summer sounds, noisy sounds, and quiet sounds.

Tomi Ungerer's almost wordless picturebook *Snail, Where Are You?* invites children to search for the hidden snail in each picture. The often-elusive snail appears in a wave, a jester's hat, as a pig's tail, and as a curl of smoke, and in many other unusual places. It's sometimes big, sometimes small but always fun to look for. Your child can also look for hidden animals in Jose Aruego and Ariane Dewey's *We Hide, You Seek*.

In Stephen Lewis' *Zoo City* your two-year-old can search for the animal on the bottom half of the split page that looks like the "city animal" on the top half. For instance, a crane and a giraffe, a wheel and a starfish, and a fire hydrant and a frog. And, as the pages are matched correctly, the animals' names appear opposite their pictures, making *Zoo City* a book that can grow with your child.

Tana Hoban, an outstanding photographer and filmmaker whose striking photos have been exhibited at the New York Museum of Modern Art, has created several superb books that invite children to actively participate. *Shapes and Things* is an identification game book that will help sharpen a child's classification skills. Featuring white silhouettes against a black background, objects are arranged in sets such as kitchen utensils and tools.

Look Again and *Take Another Look* are original picturebooks that encourage young viewers to do just as their titles say. Square and circular openings cut before each black and white photograph reveal only a tiny portion of each picture, challenging children to guess if a turtle, a daisy, an apple, an umbrella, or another familiar object awaits them on the next page. Along with heightening perceptual skills, this clever format also encourages page turning and builds vocabulary.

Two-year-olds delight in the sounds of words and respond readily to books full of onomatopoeia, the use of words that sound like what they mean (for example, snap, crackle, and pop). My young students call such books "sound books," and their favorites include Peter Spier's *Crash! Bang! Boom!* and *Gobble, Growl, Grunt* and Karla Kuskin's *Roar and More*, which all invite both participation and imitation.

Ruth Krauss' *Bears* is another favorite. Each large-sized page shows playful bears doing some very unbearlike things that include "washing hairs, giving stares, collecting fares, stepping in squares."

CONCEPT BOOKS

Now is the time to use simple concept books to begin actively teaching your child basic concepts such as the alphabet, counting, colors, and shapes.

Celestino Piatti's Animals ABC is an appropriate ABC book because it features big, bold, capital letters, colorful, boldly outlined illustrations, and humorous verses. For instance, "The whale grins and floats/And churns the sea/Then spouts a cup of salty tea." The double-page spreads of a giraffe, a whale, and the clever "X" animal are special attractions of this large-format book. Anne Alexander's *The ABC of Cars and Trucks* and Fritz Eichenberg's *Ape in a Cape: An Alphabet of Odd Animals* are also popular, and their titles alone explain their wide appeal. Also appealing is *Apples to Zippers: An Alphabet Book* by Patricia Ruben. Its engaging black and white photos of people, animals, and things complement bold upper- and lower-case letters and words describing the actions in the pictures.

Favorite counting books include Nina Sazer's *What Do You Think I Saw?*, a nonsense number book that playfully describes in rhyme the fanciful creatures a pink rhinoceros sees on her way to town one day. For instance, "two pink llamas in purple pajamas dancing around on their toes." As it reinforces counting up to ten with large, colorful numerals at the upper left-hand side of each double-page spread, this humorous book also introduces rhyming words and some very unusual jellybean-colored animals.

Maurice Sendak's *Seven Little Monsters* is also popular. This whimsical counting book stars comical creatures who eat tulip trees, drink tumbling seas, and other absurdities. Unfortunately, the numerals are not depicted in this silly counting and rhyme book.

Susanna Gretz' *Teddy Bears 1-10* features huggable love-worn bears (aren't they all?) who undergo a wonderful transformation. The illustration of four bears swishing around in a washing machine always produces shrieks of laughter, and each colorful full-page picture is accompanied by a large numeral and bold-faced text describing the action.

Noteworthy color books include Dick Bruna's simple *My Shirt Is White*, which teaches not only colors but articles of clothing; Eric Carle's *My Very First Book of Colors*, a board book which invites children to find the object on the bottom half of the split page that matches the color on the top half; and Tana Hoban's *Is It Red? Is It Yellow? Is It Blue?*, a stunning book that, unlike the typical name-the-color books, also teaches about shapes, sizes, relationships, and textures. The predominant colors in each large color photograph are indicated by a row of corresponding circles beneath the picture and tempt young viewers to look and look again. Most importantly, *Is It Red? Is It Yellow? Is It Blue?* also invites children to notice and appreciate the beauty in ordinary objects, from a stack of plastic milk crates to a discarded umbrella.

Tana Hoban has also created an especially good concept book about shapes. Through its black and white photographs, *Circles, Triangles, and Squares* gives viewers an exciting glimpse at everyday city sights—children blowing bubbles, tying sneakers, spinning hoops, and a subway train zooming by a bridge—as it teaches basic geometric shapes. The object of this book is to search for the shapes in each picture. The lesson? Shapes are all around us just waiting to be discovered!

Ed Emberley's *The Wing on a Flea* and Eric Carle's split-matching book *My Very First Book of Shapes*, in which children match a kite with a rectangle, a teepee with a triangle, and a watermelon slice with a semi-circle, are also worth a look.

Perhaps your two-year-old will also enjoy some of the books discussed in the next chapter, so look ahead and explore picturebooks about the "real" world, reassuring books, realistic stories, more wordless books, and traditional nursery tales.

BOOKS FOR TWO-YEAR-OLDS

Books listed at the end of Chapters 1 and 2 will still be suitable now, and some two-year-olds will be ready for books at the end of Chapter 4, so don't limit yourself to just one list.

For easy reference, the books are grouped thematically and alphabetized according to authors. Those mentioned within this chapter are marked with an asterisk (*).

Simple Storybooks

*Ets, Marie Hall. *In the Forest.* Viking, 1944.

*———*Gilberto and the Wind.* Viking, 1963.

*———*Just Me.* Viking, 1965.

*———*Play With Me.* Viking, 1955.

Fujikawa, Gyo. *Oh, What a Busy Day.* Grosset & Dunlap, 1976.

Hutchins, Pat. *Rosie's Walk.* Macmillan, 1968.

*Keats, Ezra Jack. *The Snowy Day.* Viking, 1962.

Kraus, Robert. *Milton the Early Riser.* Jose Aruego and Ariane Dewey, ill. Windmill/Simon & Schuster, 1972.

———*Owliver.* Jose Aruego and Ariane Dewey, ill. Windmill/Simon & Schuster, 1974.

Krauss, Ruth. *A Hole Is to Dig.* Maurice Sendak, ill. Harper, 1952.

———*The Carrot Seed.* Crockett Johnson, ill. Harper, 1945.

McCloskey, Robert. *Blueberries for Sal.* Viking, 1948.

Mitchell, Cynthia. *Playtime.* Satomi Ichikawa, ill. Philomel, 1979.

*Preston, Edna Mitchell. *The Temper Tantrum Book.* Rainey Bennet, ill. Viking, 1976.

*Rice, Eve. *Oh Lewis!* Macmillan, 1974.

———*What Sadie Sang.* Greenwillow, 1976.

Watanabe, Shigeo. *Get Set! Go!* Yasuo Ohtomo, ill. Philomel, 1981.

———*How Do I Put It On?* Yasuo Ohtomo, ill. Philomel, 1979.

———*What a Good Lunch!* Yasuo Ohtomo, ill. Philomel, 1980.

Watson, Wendy. *Jamie's Story.* Philomel, 1981.

Zolotow, Charlotte. *One Step, Two...* Cindy Wheeler, ill. Lothrop, 1980.

———*William's Doll.* William Pene Du Bois, ill. Harper, 1972.

Wordless Books

Hogrogian, Nonny. *Apples.* Macmillan, 1972.

*Hutchins, Pat. *Changes, Changes.* Macmillan, 1971.

Keats, Ezra Jack. *Kitten for a Day.* Watts, 1974.

———*Pssst! Doggie.* Watts, 1973.

———*Skates!* Watts, 1973; Four Winds, 1981.

Lisowski, Gabriel. *The Invitation.* Holt, 1980.

*Mayer, Mercer. *Ah-Choo.* Dial, 1976.

*———*Bubble, Bubble.* Four Winds, 1973.

*———*Hiccup.* Dial, 1976.

*———*Oops.* Dial, 1977.

*Turkle, Brinton. *Deep in the Forest.* Dutton, 1976.

Participation or Response Books

*Aruego, Jose and Ariane Dewey. *We Hide, You Seek.* Greenwillow, 1979.

*Brown, Margaret Wise. *The Country Noisy Book.* Leonard Weisgard, ill. Harper, 1940.

*——— *The (City) Noisy Book.* Leonard Weisgard, ill. Harper, 1939.

*——— *The Quiet Noisy Book.* Leonard Weisgard, ill. Harper, 1950.

*——— *The Summer Noisy Book.* Charles Shaw, ill. Harper, 1951.

*——— *The Winter Noisy Book.* Charles Shaw, ill. Harper, 1947.

——— *Where Have You Been?* Barbara Cooney, ill. Hastings, 1963.

Eastman, P. D. *Are You My Mother?* Random House, 1960.

Hoban, Tana. *Dig Drill, Dump Fill.* Greenwillow, 1975.

*——— *Look Again.* Macmillan, 1971.

*——— *Shapes and Things.* Macmillan, 1970.

*——— *Take Another Look.* Greenwillow, 1981.

——— *Where Is It?* Macmillan, 1974.

Kraus, Robert. *Whose Mouse Are You?* Jose Aruego, ill. Macmillan, 1940.

*Krauss, Ruth. *Bears.* Phyllis Rowand, ill. Harper, 1948.

*Kuskin, Karla. *Roar and More.* Harper, 1956.

*Lewis, Stephen. *Zoo City.* Greenwillow, 1976.

Livermore, Elaine. *Find the Cat.* Houghton Mifflin, 1973.

——— *Lost and Found.* Houghton Mifflin, 1975.

——— *One to Ten, Count Again.* Houghton Mifflin, 1973.

——— *Three Little Kittens.* Houghton Mifflin, 1979.

Munari, Bruno. *Who's There? Open the Door.* Philomel, 1980.

Shaw, Charles G. *It Looked Like Spilt Milk.* Harper, 1947.

*Spier, Peter. *Crash! Bang! Boom!* Doubleday, 1972.

*——— *Gobble, Growl, Grunt.* Doubleday, 1971.

Ungerer, Tomi. *One, Two, Where's My Shoe?* Harper, 1964.

*——— *Snail, Where Are You?* Harper, 1962.

Zacharias, Thomas. *But Where Is the Green Parrot?* Delacorte, 1978.

Concept Books
ABC Books

*Alexander, Anne. *The ABC of Cars and Trucks.* Doubleday, 1971.

Crowther, Robert. *The Most Amazing Hide and Seek Alphabet Book.* Viking, 1978.

*Eichenberg, Fritz. *Ape in a Cape: An Alphabet of Odd Animals.* Harcourt, 1952.

Greenaway, Kate. *A Apple Pie.* Warne, 1886.

Gretz, Susanna. *Teddy Bears ABC.* Follett, 1975.

Oxenbury, Helen. *Helen Oxenbury's ABC of Things.* Watts, 1972.

*Piatti, Celestino. *Celestino Piatti's Animal ABC.* Atheneum, 1966.

Rey, H. A. *Curious George Learns the Alphabet.* Houghton Mifflin, 1963.

*Ruben, Patricia. *Apples to Zippers: An Alphabet Book.* Doubleday, 1976.
Sedgwick, Paulita. *Circus ABC.* Holt, 1978.
Sendak, Maurice. *Alligators All Around (Nutshell Library).* Harper, 1962.

Number Books

Eichenberg, Fritz. *Dancing in the Moon.* Harcourt, 1956.
Ginsberg, Mirra. *Kitten from One to Ten.* Guilio Maestro, ill. Crown, 1981.
*Gretz, Susanna. *Teddy Bears 1-10.* Follett, 1968.
Holl, Adelaide. *Let's Count.* Lucinda McQueen, ill. Addison-Wesley, 1976.
Keats, Ezra Jack. *Over in the Meadow.* Parents, 1979.
Oxenbury, Helen. *Numbers of Things.* Watts, 1968.
Reiss, John. *Numbers.* Bradbury, 1971.
*Sazer, Nina. *What Do You Think I Saw? A Nonsense Number Book.* Lois Ehlert, ill. Pantheon, 1976.
*Sendak, Maurice. *Seven Little Monsters.* Harper, 1975.
———*One Was Johnny (Nutshell Library).* Harper, 1962.

Color Books

*Bruna, Dick. *My Shirt Is White.* Methuen.
*Carle, Eric. *My Very First Book of Colors.* Crowell, 1974.
Freeman, Don. *The Chalk Box Story.* Lippincott, 1976.
*Hoban, Tana. *Is It Red? Is It Yellow? Is It Blue?* Greenwillow, 1978.
Reiss, John. *Colors.* Bradbury, 1969.
Rossetti, Christina. *What Is Pink?* Jose Aruego, ill. Macmillan, 1971.

Shape Books

*Carle, Eric. *My Very First Book of Shapes.* Crowell, 1974.
*Emberley, Ed. *The Wing on a Flea.* Little Brown, 1961.
*Hoban, Tana. *Circles, Triangles, and Squares.* Macmillan, 1974.
Reiss, John. *Shapes.* Bradbury, 1974.
Schlein, Miriam. *Shapes.* Addison-Wesley, 1952.

CHAPTER 4
AGES THREE TO FOUR

*For the children and the flowers are
my sisters and my brothers,
Their laughter and their loveliness
could clear a cloudy day.
Like the music of the mountains and
the colors of the rainbow,
They're a promise for the future and
a blessing for today.
—John Denver
"Rhymes and Reasons"*

No longer a toddler, just on the brink of becoming a preschooler, your three-year-old is wide-eyed, curious, talkative, always questioning, wondering, and reaching.

Although your three-year-old will still enjoy many books that younger children enjoy, his experiences are greater, creating a need for more variety in books. Since your adventurous three-year-old is now reaching out into her ever-expanding world with extended arms (and an extending attention span) and is eager to know about the "real" world, picturebooks about people at work, animals, and vehicles are all appropriate as are reassuring books, realistic books, more sophisticated wordless books, and traditional nursery stories.

BOOKS ABOUT THE "REAL"WORLD

Several books by Harlow and Anne Rockwell can help your child explore the "real" world. The hallmark of the Rockwells' books is simplicity; their illustrations are bold and clear, and their texts are sparse—a perfect combination for young children. *My Kitchen* introduces many recognizable culinary objects, while *The Supermarket* features a multitude of brightly colored grocery items that invite identification. And in *My Doctor, My Dentist,* and *My Barber,* three potentially frightening experiences are painlessly previewed. Each of these picturebooks succeeds in assuaging children's apprehensions as they explain through simple pictures and text what can be expected during routine visits. I especially like the fact that Rockwell's doctor is female.

With Peter Spier's *Village Books* your three-year-old can visit a nursery school, pet store, food market, firehouse, toy shop, and service station. Each of these books is die-cut in the shape of a building and, since they are made of sturdy laminated board material, your child can stand them up to make a village. Spier's realistic, detail-filled illustrations are

Reprinted by permission of Philomel Books, a division of the Putnam Publishing Group, from *A Very Hungry Caterpillar* by Eric Carle.

matched by simple texts that introduce vocabularies appropriate to six very different environments.

Introduce your child to females doing many kinds of jobs in Eve Merriam's *Mommies at Work*, a modern classic in which your child will meet dancer mommies, writer mommies, cashier mommies, and assembly-line mommies who also make cookies, tie shoelaces, and have laps to snuggle in. Your child will be delighted to learn that all these mommies love best of all "to be your very own mommy, and come home to you!"

Another book that realistically shows women at work is Wendy Saul's *Butcher, Baker, Cabinetmaker: Photographs of Women at Work*. This collection of striking black and white photos complemented by a simple text introduces children to women of various backgrounds who work at nontraditional jobs. Sure to provoke discussion, this book is aimed at heightening your child's awareness of women's potential, and, unlike other books of its kind, also encourages your child to look more closely at photographs.

Animals always seem to fascinate children—probably because they are just as uninhibited, curious, and lovable as children themselves. Picturebooks about animals are numerous, and Brian Wildsmith's are among the most popular. Their large formats and bright illustrations are undoubtedly appealing. *Fishes, Birds, Squirrels, Wild Animals, Animal Games,* and *Animal Homes* all deserve a look. Favorite animal books in my preschool classes include Eric Carle's *The Very Hungry Caterpillar* and Ruth Krauss' *The Happy Day*. In Carle's book your child can accompany a very hungry caterpillar as he eats his way through one apple on Monday, two pears on Tuesday, three plums on Wednesday, and so on until he miraculously becomes a beautiful butterfly in the final picture. Besides telling the amazing story of metamorphosis, this innovative picturebook also reinforces the concepts of naming the days of the week and counting up to ten. Your child will love the cleverly die-cut, "caterpillar-eaten-through" pages and will enjoy analyzing and mimicking the caterpillar's various facial expressions, especially his "bellyache" look after having eaten an astonishing variety and quantity of food.

In Krauss' 1949 classic, forest animals awake from their long winter's sleep to discover the joyous coming of spring. Especially appealing are this book's large format; simple, repetitive text; and full-page, snow-speckled, black and white illustrations of field mice, snails, squirrels, bears, and ground hogs in their natural habitats. The single, bright touch of color in a flower that the animals discover at the book's conclusion is a welcomed surprise for the animals and for your child.

Like animals, books about vehicles are always winners. Donald Crews' *Truck*, which stars a huge, red rig carrying a shipment of bicycles over bridges, on superhighways, and through tunnels in an assortment of weather conditions, and *Freight Train*, in which a multicolored train speeds across the pages and trains a child's eyes to move from left to right (an essential reading readiness skill), are especially popular. Other favorites include Watty Piper's *The Little Engine That Could*, in which a tiny engine pulls a trainful of toys up a mountain to the refrain of "I think I can, I think I can, I think I can"; Hardie Gramatky's *Little Toot*, the saga of a New York harbor tugboat that becomes a hero in time of crisis; Virginia Lee Burton's *Katy and the Big Snow*, the story of a red crawler tractor who plows out an entire blizzard-covered town; and *Mike Mulligan and His Steam Shovel*, the tale of a spunky steam shovel named Mary Anne who digs out a basement and finds a new home and job for herself. Each of these classics has delighted generations of children and is sure to delight your three-year-old too. Interestingly, all of these books share the theme of achievement and ultimate acceptance. The Little Engine, Little Toot, Katy, and Mary Anne all overcome obstacles and succeed in accomplishing a seemingly impossible task. It is this theme that has made these picturebooks true classics and will make them favorites for your child. After all, three-year-olds are achievers who like to identify with the underdog. They welcome and need books that encourage their independence and celebrate their competency.

REASSURING BOOKS

Three heralds the beginning of imaginative, cooperative play and a blossoming self-image. Yet, although your three-year-old revels in newfound freedom and emerging independence, she also realizes that growing up is often difficult (especially if growing up includes going off to nursery school and accepting the arrival of a new sibling). Three-year-olds need and enjoy simple stories that provide comfort and reassurance, stories that foster a positive self-image.

One of my favorite "comfort books" is Ruth Bornstein's *Little Gorilla*, a perfect read-aloud story especially if you hold your child lovingly in your lap while sharing it. Little Gorilla is

From the book *Little Gorilla* by Ruth Bornstein, published by Clarion Books, Ticknor & Fields:
A Houghton Mifflin Company, New York. Copyright © 1976 by Ruth Bornstein.

loved by everyone in the great green forest—his mother, his father, his aunts and uncles, all his animal friends—even when he's not so little anymore. Every time I share this story with a child, my listener's eyes inevitably widen with apprehension at the words, "And one day something happened... Little Gorilla began to grow and grow and grow..." But, when Little Gorilla is loved even when he's older (and bigger!), there's always a sigh of relief. *Little Gorilla* is so well-loved by my preschoolers that I use it as a special "birthday book" and read it each time one of my students celebrates a birthday.

Margaret Wise Brown's classic *The Runaway Bunny*, which tells of the adventures of a bunny who plays a fanciful game of hide and seek with his mother, is another favorite. This imaginative bunny pretends that he is going to become a fish, a mountain climber, a crocus, a bird, a sailboat, a tightrope walker, and a little boy in his attempts to run away, but his ingenious mother always finds him and promises that she will catch him in her arms and hug him. This reassuring book ends with mother and "child" cozy in their rabbit hole, sharing a carrot.

Don Freeman's *Corduroy* is another book that provides security and reassurance for young children. This popular story of a department store teddy bear with an adventuresome spirit and a missing button on his overalls proves that one need not be perfect to be loved.

Millions of Cats by Wanda Gag delivers a similar message to young listeners as it tells of a couple who wanted one cat but find themselves with "millions and billions and trillions of cats!" Jealous over who is the prettiest, the cats destroy each other, but one, thin, scraggly kitten survives because he is so homely that no one even bothered with him. Young children identify with this kitten who becomes beautiful when he is loved and taken care of. The rhythmic quality of Gag's text and her flowing black and white illustrations have made this 1928 book a classic.

Another picturebook that successfully bolsters sagging little egos is Barbara William's *Someday Said Mitchell.* "Someday I will be big. Then I will take care of you," promises little Mitchell to his busy mother. His sensitive mother assures Mitchell that he can help her now, even though he's little. Kay Chorao, one of my favorite illustrators, has filled her delicate, pencil drawings with amusing details and has gently captured the love between mother and child in their realistic facial expressions. Perhaps the pictures of little Mitchell happily dusting a chair and eagerly reaching inside a grocery bag will induce your little one to lend a helping hand too.

BOOKS ABOUT SCHOOL AND A NEW BABY

As if leaving toddlerhood isn't hard enough, three-year-olds are often faced with the challenges of adjusting to nursery school and accepting the arrival of a new brother or sister as well. Picturebooks about these and other threatening situations can help lessen apprehensions and, most importantly, can help open up the channel of communication between you and your child. This is called bibliotherapy, the use of books as therapy, and countless studies have proven that certain books can indeed help in times of stress. So select realistic books wisely and use them as tools to help your child adjust to new situations such as going to nursery school and accepting a new sibling. (See Chapter 5 for more bibliotherapeutic books.)

Many children about to enter the unfamiliar world of a nursery school or day-care center are afraid and insecure. Appropriately chosen picturebooks can comfort, reassure, and familiarize your child with the everyday happenings at school. Ideally, these books will not only reduce your child's apprehensions but yours, too, by accentuating the objectives and values of early childhood education.

My Nursery School by the master of simplicity, Harlow Rockwell, is an uncluttered book in which a little girl excitedly describes the various activities at her school. The childlike text—"First I will play with the clay. I will punch it and poke it and squeeze it and roll it flat ..."—is matched by colorful pictures. In Rockwell's nonsexist, multiracial classroom, your child will find both a male and female teacher, a boy wheeling a doll carriage, a girl building a tower, a boy hugging a teddy bear, a girl riding a fire engine, a boy cutting and pasting paper, and a girl driving a bulldozer through a pan of cornmeal. While his setting is highly realistic, Rockwell's ratio of two teachers to ten children, however, is very unrealistic.

Miriam Cohen's *Will I Have a Friend?* humorously supplies an answer to that often-asked question as it follows the school day through arts and crafts time, snack, story, nap, and playtime. Soft illustrations of rather pudgy racially mixed children complement the story.

In Kay Chorao's *Molly's Lies,* your three-year-old will empathize with Molly who, on her first day of school, stuffs her new red jumper into the wastebasket and tells her mother it got "lost." Molly saves her most elaborate lie for school where she tells Joseph, her new class-mate, all about her pet crocodile who lives in her closet and eats chocolate raisins! This sensitive and witty story about an imaginative yet insecure child who finally overcomes her fear is highlighted by Chorao's characteristically detailed illustrations. My preschoolers especially liked the picture on the back cover that reveals a smiling crocodile peering out of Molly's closet!

Bill Bizen's *First Day in School* is a realistic introductory book. The expressions of the children featured in Bizen's black and white photos capture their insecurity, apprehension, and reluctance to enter the strange world of school. They nervously cling to their mothers, listlessly lean against doorways, sorrowfully sulk in their new classrooms, and, inevitably, cry. But your child will be comforted in knowing that it isn't long before their teacher "makes [them] feel at home" and they all become busily involved in the activities of the day.

Edith Thacher Hurd's *Come With Me to Nursery School,* which was created especially to help parents answer the question, "What will I do at my school?" is undoubtedly one of the best books of its kind. Edward Bigelow's nonsexist, black and white photographs of multira-cial children are superbly complemented by a text written with sensitivity and an acute awareness of the needs and feelings of young children. For instance: "There are slides for sliding. At first it seems a bit scary. But after a while it's not scary at all." And, "Bang! Bang! Bang! There is lots of noise when we make things with hammer and nails... But sometimes we do quiet things. If you blow and blow, bubbles grow out of the water and float away. Sometimes it's nice just to sit and watch what other people are doing." And, "At my school we can draw whatever we like. It's fun to paint pictures. But sometimes it's hard to know what color to choose. Red, green or yellow, which would we use?" Hurd's text not only describes preschool activities but also poses appropriate questions to young listeners, encouraging participation and emphasizing that there is room for each child's unique indi-viduality and creativity in the school environment.

When a new baby arrives in your family, Ann Herbert Scott's *On Mother's Lap* can help alleviate jealousy and soften the shock by lovingly reassuring your three-year-old that he is still important. Your child will identify with Michael, a little Eskimo boy, as he and "Baby both snuggled close to Mother. Boat and Dolly and Puppy were in Michael's arms, the reindeer blanket wrapped around them all. Back and forth, back and forth they rocked." Bold illustrations of this affectionate family enhance a simple, gentle text that proves that "there's always room on Mother's lap" and in her heart.

Another favorite "welcome-the-baby" book is Ezra Jack Keats' *Peter's Chair,* which humorously portrays a little boy's jealousy upon seeing his very own cradle, highchair, and crib painted pink for his new sister. After discovering that he no longer fits in his once-favorite chair, Peter realizes that he is growing up and eventually comes to accept his baby sister and his new place in the family.

Like Peter, Frances the badger also undergoes a change in Russell Hoban's *A Baby Sister for Frances*. Poor Frances! Her mother is so busy caring for the new family addition that she doesn't iron Frances' blue dress or shop for raisins. So Frances must wear her yellow dress to school and settle for bananas on her oatmeal! Feeling rejected, this spunky little badger decides to pack her knapsack and run away. And run away she does—under the dining room table! Wise, loving parents help Frances realize that even though there's a new baby in their family, Frances is still special and unique and very much loved.

WORDLESS BOOKS

Since three is a time for increasing visual acuity and language development, now is the time for you to introduce your child to more sophisticated wordless books, although those described in the previous chapter can and should also be enjoyed now. Three-year-olds love to analyze, to dissect, to look at things. Nothing, including the most minute detail, will escape their scrutiny, their insatiable curiosity. It's no surprise then that they are intrigued by wordless books and love to entertain themselves and any available audience by creating their own stories to match the pictures. When presented with a wordless book, one of my preschoolers looked at it in disappointment and complained, "This book says nothing." After looking at it for a while, though, this young critic had a change of heart and excitedly whispered to me, "This book says nothing, but I can make it say a lot of things!" Your three-year-old will enjoy making the following wordless books say a lot of things, and, as he does, you should write down the story your child creates and then read it aloud. This "game" will help your child realize that print is simply written-down talk, an essential reading readiness skill.

Often-"read" wordless books in my classes include several by artist, cartoonist, filmmaker Fernando Krahn. In *How Santa Claus Had a Long and Difficult Journey Delivering His Presents*, your child will laugh at a bumbling Santa who has considerable trouble getting his toy-laden sleigh in the air, until he gets some heavenly help. And in *The Self-Made Snowman*, she can follow a lump of fallen snow as it rolls down a mountainside and becomes magically transformed into a gigantic (and distinguishedly-dressed) snowman.

Another favorite is Eric Carle's *Do You Want to Be My Friend?* in which your child can accompany a lonely little mouse as he searches for a friend. Along the way he meets many tails whose owners are revealed only after each page is turned. Imagine his surprise—and your child's—when an alligator, a lion, a hippo, a peacock, and many other animals are discovered. This fun-filled, innovative picturebook was specially designed to help children develop reading readiness skills such as page turning, following a left to right progression, and, of course, story telling.

TRADITIONAL NURSERY STORIES

As your three-year-old's attention span increases along with the ability to deal with imaginative plots, traditional nursery stories like Beatrix Potter's beloved *The Tale of Peter Rabbit* and *The Tale of Benjamin Bunny* are appropriate. Especially appealing are cumulative or repetitional folk tales like *The Gingerbread Boy, The House That Jack Built, The Three Billy Goats Gruff,* and *The Three Little Pigs,* whose simple plots build dramatically to a climax. Each of these popular tales will heighten your child's auditory discrimination and invite active participation. After all, what child can resist joining the billy goats as they "trip-trap, trip-trap" across the rickety bridge, or can keep from chanting, "Run—run—as fast as you can! You can't catch me, I'm the gingerbread man!" and "Little pig, little pig, let me in. No, not by the hair on my chinny-chin-chin. Then I'll huff, and I'll puff, and I'll blow your house in."

Don't settle for just any version of these classic folk tales. There are countless adaptations available; compare several by examining their texts (some may be abridged) and their pictures too. Each illustrator adds his or her unique interpretation and style to these stories, and, in doing so, invariably influences the impression that your child will get from the tales. For instance, Erik Blegvad's little pigs, which are delicately drawn in pen and ink and color pencils, are proper English pigs. In the opening scene, in which the pigs are sent out to seek their fortunes, one pig, dressed in knickers and carrying a knapsack, bids his smiling mother a calm farewell as he mounts his bicycle. His two similarly dressed brothers are already down the road. In contrast, Paul Galdone's version shows three, teary-eyed, naked pigs holding hobo sticks and waving a sad goodbye to their crying mother. Quite a different picture!

Have fun while comparing versions. Remember that each illustrator's rendition holds something special to be discovered; become a keen observer and encourage your child to become one also.

You may be wondering if now is a good time to introduce your child to fairy tales. While many three-year-olds may seem to enjoy stories like *Cinderella, Snow White, Sleeping Beauty,* and *Jack and the Beanstalk,* I suggest that you save most of the potentially frightening Grimms and Perrault tales for a few more years when your child will be more adept at distinguishing between fantasy and reality. The wait will be worth it, and in the meantime you can explore and enjoy a wide variety of books appropriate for your three-year-old.

BOOKS FOR THREE-YEAR-OLDS

Use this list together with the previous lists and with the list at the end of Chapter 5. For easy reference, books are grouped thematically and alphabetized by author. Those mentioned within this chapter are marked with an asterisk (*).

Books About the "Real" World
People at Work

Barton, Byron. *Building a House.* Greenwillow, 1981.

*Merriam, Eve. *Mommies at Work.* Beni Montresor, ill. Knopf, 1961.

*Rockwell, Harlow. *My Kitchen.* Greenwillow, 1980.

*——— *My Dentist.* Greenwillow, 1975.

*——— *My Doctor.* Macmillan, 1973.

*Rockwell, Anne and Harlow. *My Barber.* Macmillan, 1981.

*——— *The Supermarket.* Macmillan, 1979.

*Saul, Wendy. *Butcher, Baker, Cabinetmaker: Photographs of Women at Work.* Abigail Heyman, photo. Crowell, 1978.

*Spier, Peter. *Village Books: Bill's Service Station, The Firehouse, The Food Market, The Toy Shop, The Pet Shop, My School.* Doubleday, 1981.

Animals

*Carle, Eric. *The Very Hungry Caterpillar.* Philomel, 1974.

Flack, Marjorie. *Angus and the Cats.* Doubleday, 1931.

——— *Angus and the Ducks.* Doubleday, 1930.

——— *Ask Mr. Bear.* Macmillan, 1932.

Kessler, Ethel and Leonard. *Do Baby Bears Sit in Chairs?* Doubleday, 1961.

*Krauss, Ruth. *The Happy Day.* Marc Simont, ill. Harper, 1949.

Leaf, Munro. *The Story of Ferdinand.* Robert Lawson, ill. Viking, 1936.

Lionni, Leo. *Fish Is Fish.* Pantheon, 1970.

——— *Swimmy.* Pantheon, 1963.

Munari, Bruno. *Bruno Munari's Zoo.* World, 1963.

Noguere, Suzanne and Tony Chen. *Little Koala.* Tony Chen, ill. Holt, 1979.

Rice, Eve. *Sam Who Never Forgets.* Greenwillow, 1977.

*Wildsmith, Brian. *Animal Games.* Oxford University Press, 1980.

*——— *Animal Homes.* Oxford University Press, 1980.

*——— *Birds.* Oxford University Press, 1980.

*——— *Fishes.* Watts, 1968.

*——— *Squirrels.* Watts, 1975.

*——— *Wild Animals.* Oxford University Press, 1980.

Williams, Garth. *The Rabbit's Wedding.* Harper, 1958.

Zalben, Jane Breskin. *Will You Count the Stars Without Me?* Farrar, 1979.

Vehicles

Burton, Virginia Lee. *Choo Choo.* Houghton Mifflin, 1937.

*——— *Katy and the Big Snow.* Houghton Mifflin, 1943.

——— *Maybelle, the Cable Car.* Houghton Mifflin, 1952.

*———*Mike Mulligan and His Steam Shovel.* Houghton Mifflin, 1939.

*Crews, Donald. *Freight Train.* Greenwillow, 1978.

*———*Truck.* Greenwillow, 1980.

Gibbons, Gail. *Trucks.* Crowell, 1981.

*Gramatky, Hardie. *Little Toot.* Putnam, 1939.

Lenski, Lois. *The Little Airplane.* Walck, 1938.

———*The Little Auto.* Walck, 1934.

———*The Little Sailboat.* Walck, 1937.

———*The Little Train.* Walck, 1940.

*Piper, Watty. *The Little Engine That Could.* George and Doris Hauman, ill. Platt & Munk, 1961.

Reassuring Books

*Bornstein, Ruth. *Little Gorilla.* Seabury, 1976.

*Brown, Margaret Wise. *The Runaway Bunny.* Clement Hurd, ill. Harper, 1942.

*Freeman, Don. *Corduroy.* Viking, 1968.

———*A Pocket for Corduroy.* Viking, 1978.

*Gag, Wanda. *Millions of Cats.* Coward, 1928.

*Williams, Barbara. *Someday Said Mitchell.* Kay Chorao, ill. Dutton, 1976.

Yashima, Taro. *Umbrella.* Viking, 1958.

Books About School

*Bizen, Bill. *First Day in School.* Doubleday, 1972.

*Chorao, Kay. *Molly's Lies.* Seabury, 1979.

*Cohen, Miriam. *Will I Have a Friend?* Lillian Hoban, ill. Macmillan, 1967.

*Hurd, Edith Thacher. *Come With Me to Nursery School.* Edward Bigelow, photo. Coward, 1970.

Kantrowitz, Mildred. *Willy Bear.* Nancy Winslow Parker, ill. Four Winds, 1980.

*Rockwell, Harlow. *My Nursery School.* Greenwillow, 1976.

Surowiecki, Sandra. *Joshua's Day.* Patricia Riley Lenthall, ill. Lollipop Power, 1972.

Books About a New Baby

Alexander, Martha. *Nobody Asked Me If I Wanted a Baby Sister.* Dial, 1971.

———*When the Baby Comes, I'm Moving Out.* Dial, 1979.

Hazen, Barbara Shook. *Gorilla Wants to be the Baby.* Jacqueline Smith, ill. Atheneum, 1978.

*Hoban, Russell. *A Baby Sister for Frances.* Lillian Hoban, ill. Harper, 1964.

Jarrell, Mary. *The Knee-Baby.* Symeon Shimin, ill. Farrar, 1973.

*Keats, Ezra Jack. *Peter's Chair.* Harper, 1967.

*Scott, Ann Herbert. *On Mother's Lap.* Glo Coalson, ill. McGraw, 1972.

Stein, Sara Bonnett. *That New Baby.* Dick Frank, photo. Walker, 1974.

Wordless Books

Alexander, Martha. *Bobo's Dream*. Dial, 1970.

———*Out, Out, Out*. Dial, 1968.

Anno, Mitsumasa. *Topsy-Turvies: Pictures to Stretch the Imagination*. Weatherhill, 1970.

Arnosky, James. *Mud Time and More—Nathaniel Stories*. Addison-Wesley, 1981.

———*Nathaniel*. Addison-Wesley, 1981.

Aruego, Jose. *Look What I Can Do*. Scribner's, 1971.

*Carle, Eric. *Do You Want to Be My Friend?* Crowell, 1971, 1981 (repub.).

———*I See a Song*. Crowell, 1973, 1981 (repub.).

Goodall, John. *Jacko*. Harcourt, 1972.

———*The Midnight Adventures of Kelly, Dot, and Esmeralda*. Atheneum, 1973.

———*Paddy's Evening Out*. Atheneum, 1973.

———*The Surprise Picnic*. Atheneum, 1977.

Krahn, Fernando. *April Fools*. Dutton, 1974.

———*The Biggest Christmas Tree on Earth*. Little Brown, 1978.

———*Here Comes Alex Pumpernickel!* Little Brown, 1981.

*———*How Santa Claus Had a Long and Difficult Journey Delivering His Presents*. Delacorte, 1970.

———*Little Love Story*. Lippincott, 1976.

*———*The Self-Made Snowman*. Lippincott, 1974.

Mayer, Mercer and Marianna. *A Boy, A Dog and A Frog*. Dial, 1967.

———*A Boy, A Dog, A Frog and A Friend*. Dial, 1978.

———*Frog, Where Are You?* Dial, 1969.

Spier, Peter. *Noah's Ark*. Doubleday, 1977.

Traditional Nursery Tales

*Asbjorsen, Peter. *The Three Billy Goats Gruff*. Paul Galdone, ill. Houghton Mifflin, 1973.

*———*The Three Billy Goats Gruff*. Marcia Brown, ill. Harcourt, 1957.

*Caldecott, Randolph, ill. *The House That Jack Built*. Watts, 1967.

Cauley, Lorinda Bryan, ad. and ill. *Goldilocks and the Three Bears*. Putnam, 1981.

Diamond, Donna, ad. and ill. *The Bremen Town Musicians*. Delacorte, 1981.

*Galdone, Paul, ad. and ill. *The Gingerbread Boy*. Houghton Mifflin, 1975.

———*The House That Jack Built*. McGraw, 1961.

Grimm, Jacob and Wilhelm. *The Bremen Town Musicians*. Elizabeth Shub, trans. Janina Domanska, ill. Greenwillow, 1980.

*Jacobs, Joseph. *The Story of the Three Little Pigs*. Lorinda Bryan Cauley, ill. Putnam, 1980.

*———*The Three Little Pigs*. Erik Blegvad, ill. Atheneum, 1980.

*———*The Three Little Pigs*. Paul Galdone, ill. Houghton Mifflin, 1970.

*Potter, Beatrix. *The Tale of Benjamin Bunny*. Warne, 1904.

*———*The Tale of Peter Rabbit*. Warne, 1902.

CHAPTER 5
AGES FOUR TO FIVE

I can hardly wait
To see you come of age
But I guess we'll both
Just have to be patient
It's a long way to go
A hard row to hoe
Yes it's a long way to go
But in the meantime
Before you cross the street ·
Take my hand
Life is what happens to you
While you're busy
Making other plans.
—John Lennon
"Beautiful Boy"

Four-year-olds can hardly wait to grow up, and, in the attempt to speed up the process, they love to dress up and role-play, magically transforming themselves into mommies, daddies, grandpas, grandmas, teachers, and clowns. Four-year-olds are imaginative, gregarious, exuberant, and wonderful. Since they have increasing attention spans, four-year-olds are generally good listeners and enjoy a wide array of stories with fanciful, dramatic plots, especially funny and scary stories. Now is also an appropriate time for books about stressful situations, picturebooks with varied artistic styles, and sophisticated concept books.

HUMOROUS BOOKS

Although four-year-olds can be spellbound by a large variety of books, they especially enjoy humorous books with unexpected, outrageous, chaotic situations; books with funny characters who are easy to identify with; and books in which words are used in an amusing way.

The utter ridiculousness of Judi Barrett's *Cloudy With a Chance of Meatballs* makes it a favorite with this age group. In this hilarious tale, your four-year-old will be transported to the Land of Chewandswallow where no one cooks because all meals magically come from the sky. Large, cross-hatched illustrations show the sky raining soup and peas, snowing mashed potatoes, and storming hamburgers. The menu is always a surprise but not always a pleasant one, and your child will roar with laughter when the weather takes a turn for the worse!

Other popular books are Esphyr Slobodkina's classic *Caps for Sale,* the outrageous story of a sleepy peddler wearing a tower of caps and some very mischievous, mimicking monkeys; and Barbara Williams' *Albert's Toothache,* the tale of a toothless turtle with a toothache in his toe. A more recently published favorite that has all the ingredients of a classic is Judith Viorst's *Alexander and the Terrible, Horrible, No Good, Very Bad Day.* Forlorn Alexander comically proves that some days just nothing goes right and vows to move to Australia in search of a better day. Just the mere mention of this book's title has my prekindergarteners laughing and eager to hear about Alexander's misfortunes. And, of course, they excitedly (and often loudly) join in on the refrain, "I could tell it was going to be a terrible, horrible, no good, very bad day!"

Other funny and easy-to-identify-with characters like Alexander are Curious George, the lovable monkey who gets in and out of an assortment of odd predicaments in H. A. and Margaret Rey's well-known books; Madeline, the roguish heroine of Ludwig Bemelmans' series; Molly of Kay Chorao's *Molly's Moe;* and Frances, the obstinate badger who won't eat anything else but bread and jam in Russell Hoban's *Bread and Jam for Frances.*

Since four-year-olds are attentive to words, they generally appreciate rhymes and word plays. This quality, in part, accounts for the huge popularity of Dr. Seuss' wildly absurd books like *Green Eggs and Ham, How the Grinch Stole Christmas, The Lorax,* and *Horton Hatches the Egg.* "Dr. Seuss has the cartoonist's gift for expressing a great deal of humor in a single line or word," comment Zena Sutherland and May Hill Arbuthnot in *Children and Books,* "and he has maintained the ability to create in uncluttered pictures and text the kind of humor the younger child best enjoys—endless word play, incongruous situations, much action, sure punishment for the truly wicked. His heroes win out not because of brute strength but because the usual cycle of life, gamely lived through, comes round to their side once again."

Like Seuss' rambunctious characters, Peggy Parish's Amelia Bedelia is another favorite. When she literally dresses the chicken in clothes and trims the meat with lace in *Amelia Bedelia,* children respond with chuckles to her foolish yet understandable mistake. Other books that humorously explore double meanings and homonyms are Fred Gwynne's *A Chocolate Moose for Dinner, The King Who Rained,* and *The Sixteen Hand Horse.*

SCARY BOOKS

Along with humorous books, your child will now enjoy "scary" stories, stories that explore and assuage their own fears. One of the most popular is Maurice Sendak's *Where the Wild Things Are,* in which a little boy named Max, who is sent to bed without any supper for misbehaving, dreams his way to the Land of Wild Things where he is crowned king. Content with his newfound power, Max eventually feels lonely, and he returns home to find his supper waiting for him. At first glance you may think, as many critics have, that Sendak's bizarre monsters are too fearsome looking, but remember that Max tames these creatures who represent adult authority. Most children are delighted rather than frightened by these rather ridiculous Wild Things and see Max's experience as a triumph. Sendak's text is lyrical, his Rousseaulike illustrations are magnificent, and his format is flawless.

Mercer Mayer's *There's a Nightmare in My Closet,* the tale of a little boy who befriends his

From *Clyde Monster* by Robert L. Crowe, illustrated by Kay Chorao. Text copyright © 1976 by Robert L. Crowe. Illustrations copyright © 1976 by Kay Sproat Chorao. Reprinted by permission of the publisher, E. P. Dutton.

nightmare, is another favorite. Just as comforting and funny is Robert L. Crowe's *Clyde Monster,* the story of a little monster who is afraid of the dark because he thinks human boys and girls are going to get him! Kay Chorao's illustrations of this adorable monster and his understanding parents highlight this reassuring reversal story.

Another well-loved, Chorao-illustrated monster book is Judith Viorst's *My Mama Says There Aren't Any Zombies, Ghosts, Vampires, Creatures, Demons, Monsters, Fiends, Goblins, or Things,* the saga of a little boy who fears all sorts of monsters and his mother who comforts him. They just don't exist, she assures him. Yet this child is skeptical. After all, how can he believe his mother "when she said [his] wriggly tooth would fall out Thursday, and then it stayed till Sunday after lunch" and when she brings back rum raisin even though he asked for chocolate nut! Children love to chime in on the refrain, "Sometimes even mamas make mistakes."

BOOKS FOR STRESSFUL SITUATIONS

Carefully chosen picturebooks can not only help a child cope with threatening nightmares and monsters, but can also help a child cope with potentially traumatic situations such as death, divorce, adoption, and handicaps.

When choosing special topic books, keep in mind that they must be selected with the utmost care and discretion. Having a realistic theme is simply not enough; special topic books must be *good* books *first.* They should be honest without being clinical, sensitive without being saccharine, and direct without being condescending.

Three excellent picturebooks that deal with the deaths of animals are Margaret Wise Brown's *The Dead Bird,* Judith Viorst's *The Tenth Good Thing About Barney,* and E. B. White's *Charlotte's Web.* The first book tells of four children who find a dead bird, mourn it, and then bury it. "And every day, until they forgot, they went and sang to their little dead bird and put fresh flowers on his grave." In Viorst's book a little boy grieves over the death of his cat, Barney. At his mother's suggestion he tries to think of ten good things about his pet. He can only think of nine until he plants seeds with his father and realizes that Barney will contribute to the cycle of life. In White's famous book an unselfish spider named Charlotte gives her life for her dear friend Wilbur the pig.

Part of the Open Family Series, which features one text for children and another for adults, Sara Bonnett Stein's *About Dying* discusses the deaths of a pet bird and a grandfather, candidly exploring reactions and stressing the necessity of keeping memories alive.

Also part of the Open Family Series, Stein's *On Divorce* is an insightful book written in a simple, direct style. An especially good book on this topic is Beth Goff's *Where Is Daddy? The Story of a Divorce.* Written by a psychiatric social worker, this sensitive read-aloud book explores the many feelings, including anger, confusion, hurt, loneliness, and insecurity, that threaten children during this painful time. Also appropriate is Helen Rogers' *Morris and His Brave Lion,* which poignantly reveals that separation is painful for parents too. And in Jeanne Whitehouse Peterson's *That Is That,* Emma Rose, an American Indian child, dances a "magical Come-Home dance" in hopes that her father will return. But after the spiders have made a home in his extra pair of shoes, Emma Rose begins to accept the situation and wishes her father well, wherever he is.

Realizing that families take varied forms can also help children adjust to their own family situation. Joan Drescher's *Your Family, My Family* presents all kinds of families—big ones, little ones, one-parent ones. Similarly, *All Kinds of Families* by Norma Simon introduces a full spectrum of multiracial families highlighted by tintypelike watercolor illustrations that convey a warm, loving atmosphere.

Adoption is presented casually in Susan Lapsley's *I Am Adopted*, the story of little Charles, a happy, well-adjusted child who is aware of his adoption but too preoccupied with his interests to be upset about it. Adoption is explained as a positive experience in Valentina Wasson's *The Chosen Baby*. This warm, convincing story about parents who first enthusiastically adopt a baby boy and then a girl was originally told by the author, a pediatrician, to her own adopted son, and the fact that it has been in constant demand since its first printing in 1939 is indeed testimony to its effectiveness.

Picturebooks about children with handicaps help handicapped children by giving them the opportunity to identify with their characters and situations, and these books also encourage nonhandicapped children to understand and appreciate the handicapped children that they meet.

Sara Bonnett Stein's Open Family Book *About Handicaps*, which tells of the friendship between young Matthew and Joe, who has cerebral palsy, serves as a guide in answering many of the questions that arise from fear and curiosity.

"Howie likes to watch the snow fall. He likes to eat chocolate ice-cream... But there are many things that Howie can't do at all." Joan Fassler's *Howie Helps Himself* is the triumphant story of a young boy with cerebral palsy who succeeds in a long-wished-for dream—moving his wheelchair all by himself. Similarly, Paul White's *Janet at School* focuses on the home and school activities of a five-year-old with spina bifida who, although confined to a wheelchair, emerges, like Howie, as a spirited, fun-loving child.

Noteworthy books about children with visual impairments include Palle Petersen's *Sally Can't See*, a story about twelve-year-old Sally, who although born blind, swims, rides horses, works hard at school, and leads a very full and active life; Florence Parry Heide's *Sound of Sunshine, Sound of Rain*, a sensory, lyrical description of a young boy's perceptions of his everyday surroundings; and Ada Litchfield's *A Cane in Her Hand*, which tells of a little girl's adjustment to her impairment and her relationships with her family, friends, and special teacher.

Also by Ada Litchfield, *A Button in Her Ear* is the story of a young deaf child that casually begins, "My name is Angela Perkins and I haven't always had a button in my ear." Other picturebooks that show hearing-impaired children engaged in many normal activities are Bernard Wolf's photo-story of a six-year-old called *Anna's Silent World* and Diana Peter's *Claire and Emma*, which sensitively tells about her two- and four-year-old daughters.

"My sister cannot always tell me with words what she feels. Sometimes she can't even show me with her hands. But when she is angry or happy or sad, my sister can say more with her face and shoulders than anyone else I know." In Jeanne Whitehouse Peterson's *I Have a Sister, My Sister Is Deaf*, an older sister talks about her younger sister who is deaf, emphasizing both the positive and negative. For instance, her sister cannot hear someone knocking at the door, but during a storm she can sleep soundly while her older sister is kept awake by thunder. Love and acceptance abound in this sensitive story highlighted by Deborah Ray's soft illustrations.

Sibling love and acceptance and, at times, annoyance is also the theme of Joe Lasker's *He's My Brother*, in which a boy describes the home and school experiences of his younger brother, Jaime, who is a slow learner. Although he tells about all the things Jaime can't do well like tie shoelaces and do homework, he also poignantly acknowledges Jaime's love for babies and animals. Other outstanding books about slow learners include Robert Kraus' *Leo the Late Bloomer,* in which a little tiger blooms in his own good time; Hanne Larsen's *Don't Forget Tom,* the story of a six-year-old's daily struggles, accomplishments, and pleasures; and Harriet Sobol's *My Brother Steven Is Retarded,* in which eleven-year-old Beth poignantly explains her mixed feelings about her younger brother. *Like Me* by Alan Brightman is also excellent. Its verse-text is simple, its pictures stunning, and its message a sensitive plea for understanding: "When they call me retarded./That word's all they see./Sometimes I think/They don't even see me./Sometimes I feel funny./When that word is used./Some people who use it./Seem very confused."

BOOKS WITH VARIED ARTISTIC STYLES

In a picturebook "the text can only give bones to the story," said illustrator Edward Ardizzone. "The pictures, on the other hand, must do more than just illustrate the story. They must elaborate it. Characters have to be created pictorially because there is no space to do so verbally in the text. Besides the settings and characters, the subtleties of mood and moment have to be suggested." Pictures are indeed important to children. For visually and verbally sophisticated four-year-olds, they are springboards for discussion and targets for scrutiny. Since children are so literal, pictures that depict only a portion of an object can confuse and at times upset them. For instance, young children may interpret that a person or animal is dismembered if it is not shown in its entirety. When evaluating pictures, also remember that although color is usually preferred, young children *do* like black and white illustrations too. The popularity of Wanda Gag's *Millions of Cats* and Lynd Ward's *The Biggest Bear* is undisputable testimony to this.

The world of children's book illustration is a rich and varied one. From McCloskey's stone lithographs in *Make Way for Ducklings* to Sasek's Monet and Seuratlike pictures in *This Is Paris,* from Lamorisse's realistic photographs in *The Red Balloon* to Delessert's startling, surrealistic Boschlike paintings in Ionesco's *Story Number 1* and *Story Number 2,* children's book illustrators use many different styles and techniques. Children love variety, and they love to "copy" illustrators. So introduce your four-year-old to a wide array of styles and techniques and encourage him or her to experiment. After seeing Ed Emberley's *Drummer Hoff* and Leo Lionni's *Swimmy,* which were created with woodcuts and linoleum block prints, my prekindergarteners created their own masterpieces with potato prints. They drew over black-crayoned paper with toothpicks after admiring Barbara Cooney's exquisite scratchboard illustrations in *Chanticleer and the Fox* and Frans Haachen's striking black, white, and red scratchboard pictures in *Peter and the Wolf;* they cut and pasted collages using scraps of wrapping paper, ribbon, lace, rick-rack, and tissue paper after seeing Ezra Jack Keats' vibrant collages in *Jennie's Hat* and *The Snowy Day* and Leo Lionni's in *Inch by Inch* and *Swimmy;* and they dabbled with many different kinds of paint after seeing Celestino Piatti's colorful opaque *The Happy Owls* and Beatrix Potter's delicate watercolor *Peter Rabbit.*

CONCEPT BOOKS

Although those discussed in previous chapters can and should be enjoyed now, your four-year-old is probably ready for more challenging concept books.

One outstanding ABC book is *Anno's Alphabet: An Adventure in Imagination.* True to its subtitle this unique book features capital letters carved from wood, which teasingly invite you and your child to look closely. Yes, there are "tricks" to be discovered. For instance, half of the "M" is only a mirror-image, and the "D" curves mysteriously. Also waiting to be discovered are whimsical creatures, animals, and flowers hiding in the intricate borders that beautifully frame each page.

Another original ABC book is *On Market Street,* written by Arnold Lobel and illustrated by his wife, Anita. Accompanying a child on a fantastic shopping spree, your child can walk along Market Street and meet merchants who are made of their wares. Anita Lobel, who was inspired by seventeenth century French trade engravings, has made each page a colorful visual delight.

Dorothy Schmiderer's *The Alphabeast Book,* in which each letter graphically transforms itself into an animal (for example, "i" becomes an inchworm) is popular as is *Ed Emberley's ABC,* in which animals "print" capital letters in an amazing variety of ways. For instance, one pilot-ant skywrites an "A."

Since four-year-olds are now ready for more advanced counting and for the concept of simple addition, Dick Bruna's *I Know More About Numbers,* which explains addition up to ten, and his *I Can Count More,* which includes the numbers 13 to 24, are appropriate. Other noteworthy counting books include *Anno's Counting Book,* whose simple pictures of a country scene during different seasons will invite your child to discover sets and groups and other mathematical relationships, and Nicola Bayley's *One Old Oxford Ox,* in which the numbers one to 12 are introduced by dignified animals and a nonsensical alliterative text enhanced by the author's vibrant miniature illustrations.

Charlotte Zolotow's *Mr. Rabbit and the Lovely Present* reinforces color recognition as it tells the story of a little girl who can't decide what to give her mother for her birthday. Since her mother likes red, yellow, green, and blue, a debonair rabbit supplies a practical solution.

Since four-year-olds like to mix and experiment with colors, Leo Lionni's ingenious *Little Blue and Little Yellow* is sure to delight. Illustrated entirely with blobs of color, this tale shows what inevitably happens to Little Blue and Little Yellow because of their close friendship. No doubt your four-year-old will do some blending of his own after seeing this book! Also appropriate is Ed Emberley's *Green Says Go,* which introduces primary colors and shows how they can be mixed to produce secondary colors. Emberley also discusses how colors can be mixed to produce lighter and darker shades, and, best of all, how colors can "talk."

When choosing concept books for your four-year-old, you shouldn't miss Tana Hoban's *Push Pull, Empty Full: A Book of Opposites,* which features 15 pairs of striking black and white photos, including a turtle's head in and out, two eggs broken and whole, and jigsaw pieces apart and together. Also worth a look are Hoban's *Big Ones, Little Ones,* a photo collection of adult animals and their babies, and *Over, Under, Through and Other Spatial Concepts.*

From *On Market Street*. Text copyright © 1981 by Arnold Lobel. Illustrations copyright © 1981 by Anita Lobel. Reprinted with permission of Greenwillow Books, a division of William Morrow & Company, Inc.

Eric Carle's *The Secret Birthday Message*, in which your child can help a little boy search up, down, and through multishaped pages to find his birthday surprise, is also an excellent choice. Brightly colored and die-cut like Carle's *The Very Hungry Caterpillar*, this book will encourage your child to recognize shapes and spatial and directional relationships.

Another innovative book that graphically proves that there is more than one way to look at a picture is Beau Gardner's *The Turn About, Think About, Look About Book*. What your child sees in this book's bold-patterned pictures depends on how the pages are held. For instance, when held sideways, one colorful abstract design is a teacup handle, and when turned upside down, it is transformed into a cat's tail.

Also not to be missed is Brian Wildsmith's *What the Moon Saw*, a bright picturebook that presents a series of comparisons, including a fierce lion and a timid rabbit, a heavy elephant and a light bird, and a fast cheetah and a slow tortoise.

As your child approaches kindergarten age, many of the books discussed in the next chapter will be appropriate, so look ahead to the beginning readers, poetry books, stories, and fairy tales, folk tales, and fables that should be part of every child's literary experience.

BOOKS FOR FOUR-YEAR-OLDS

Previously discussed books will still be appropriate now, and your child may also enjoy some of the books discussed in the next chapter. Books are grouped thematically and alphabetized according to author for easy reference. Those discussed in this chapter are marked with an asterisk (*).

Humorous Books

*Barrett, Judi. *Cloudy With a Chance of Meatballs*. Ron Barrett, ill. Atheneum, 1979.

———*I'm Too Small, You're Too Big*. David S. Rose, ill. Atheneum, 1981.

———*Animals Should Definitely Not Wear Clothing*. Ron Barrett, ill. Atheneum, 1970.

*Bemelmans, Ludwig. *Madeline*. Viking, 1939.

———*Madeline in London*. Viking, 1961.

———*Madeline's Rescue*. Viking, 1953.

*Chorao, Kay. *Molly's Moe*. Seabury, 1976.

*Gwynne, Fred. *A Chocolate Moose for Dinner*. Windmill/Simon & Schuster, 1976.

*———*The King Who Rained*. Windmill/Simon & Schuster, 1970.

*———*The Sixteen Hand Horse*. Windmill/Simon & Schuster, 1980.

*Hoban, Russell. *Bread and Jam for Frances*. Lillian Hoban, ill. Harper, 1964.

———*A Bargain for Frances*. Lillian Hoban, ill. Harper, 1970.

———*Best Friends for Frances*. Lillian Hoban, ill. Harper, 1969.

———*A Birthday for Frances*. Lillian Hoban, ill. Harper, 1968.

*Parish, Peggy. *Amelia Bedelia*. Fritz Seibel, ill. Harper, 1963.

———*Thank You, Amelia Bedelia*. Fritz Seibel, ill. Harper, 1964.

———*Amelia Bedelia and the Surprise Shower*. Fritz Seibel, ill. Harper, 1966.

*Rey, H.A. and Margaret. *Curious George*. Houghton Mifflin, 1941.

———*Curious George Takes a Job*. Houghton Mifflin, 1947.

———*Curious George Rides a Bike*. Houghton Mifflin, 1952.

———*Curious George Gets a Medal*. Houghton Mifflin, 1957.

————*Curious George Goes to the Hospital.* Houghton Mifflin, 1966.

Seuss, Dr. *The Cat in the Hat.* Random House, 1957.

————*The Cat in the Hat Comes Back.* Random House, 1958.

*————*Green Eggs and Ham.* Random House, 1960.

*————*How the Grinch Stole Christmas.* Random House, 1957.

*————*The Lorax.* Random House, 1971.

*————*Horton Hatches the Egg.* Random House, 1950.

*Slobodkina, Esphyr. *Caps for Sale.* Addison-Wesley, 1947.

Sutton, Jane. *What Should a Hippo Wear?* Lynn Munsinger, ill. Houghton Mifflin, 1979.

*Viorst, Judith. *Alexander and the Terrible, Horrible, No Good, Very Bad Day.* Ray Cruz, ill. Atheneum, 1972.

————*If I Were in Charge of the World and Other Worries.* Lynn Cherry, ill. Atheneum, 1981.

Waber, Bernard. *Ira Sleeps Over.* Houghton Mifflin, 1972.

————*Lyle, Lyle Crocodile.* Houghton Mifflin, 1965.

————*The House on 86th Street.* Houghton Mifflin, 1969.

————*Lovable Lyle.* Houghton Mifflin, 1969.

————*Lyle and the Birthday Party.* Houghton Mifflin, 1966.

*Williams, Barbara. *Albert's Toothache.* Kay Chorao, ill. Dutton, 1974.

Zion, Gene. *Harry the Dirty Dog.* Margaret B. Graham, ill. Harper, 1956.

Scary Books

Bonsall, Crosby. *Who's Afraid of the Dark?* Harper, 1980.

*Crowe, Robert L. *Clyde Monster.* Kay Chorao, ill. Dutton, 1976.

Harper, Wilhelmina. *The Gunniwolf.* William Weisner, ill. Dutton, 1918.

*Mayer, Mercer. *There's a Nightmare in My Closet.* Dial, 1968.

Peck, Richard. *Monster Night at Grandma's House.* Don Freeman, ill. Viking, 1981.

*Sendak, Maurice. *Where the Wild Things Are.* Harper, 1963.

*Viorst, Judith. *My Mama Says There Aren't Any Zombies, Ghosts, Vampires, Creatures, Demons, Monsters, Fiends, Goblins, or Things.* Kay Chorao, ill. Atheneum, 1973.

Books for Stressful Situations
Death

*Brown, Margaret Wise. *The Dead Bird.* Remy Charlip, ill. Addison-Wesley, 1958.

Dobrin, Arnold. *Scat.* Four Winds, 1971.

Fassler, Joan. *My Grandpa Died Today.* Stuart Kranz, ill. Human Science Press, 1971.

Miles, Miska. *Annie and the Old One.* Peter Parnell, ill. Little Brown, 1971.

*Stein, Sara Bonnett. *About Dying.* Dick Frank, photo. Walker, 1974.

*Viorst, Judith. *The Tenth Good Thing About Barney.* Erik Blegvad, ill. Atheneum, 1971.

*White, E.B. *Charlotte's Web.* Garth Williams, ill. Harper, 1952.

Zolotow, Charlotte. *My Grandson Lew.* William Pene duBois, ill. Harper, 1974.

Divorce and One-Parent Homes

Caines, Jeanette. *Daddy.* Ronald Himler, ill. Harper, 1977.

*Drescher, Joan. *Your Family, My Family.* Walker, 1980.

*Goff, Beth. *Where Is Daddy? The Story of a Divorce.* Susan Perl, ill. Beacon, 1969.

*Peterson, Jeanne Whitehouse. *That Is That.* Deborah Ray, ill. Harper, 1979.

*Rogers, Helen. *Morris and His Brave Lion.* Glo Coalson, ill. McGraw, 1975.

*Simon, Norma. *All Kinds of Families.* Joe Lasker, ill. Whitman, 1976.

Sitea, Linda. "Zachary's Divorce" in *Free to Be You and Me.* McGraw, 1974.

*Stein, Sara Bonnett. *On Divorce.* Erika Stone, photo. Walker, 1974.

Zindel, Paul. *I Love My Mother.* J. Melo, ill. Harper, 1975.

Zolotow, Charlotte. *The Summer Night.* Ben Shecter, ill. Harper, 1974.

Adoption

Bunin, Catherine and Sherry. *Is That Your Sister?* Pantheon, 1976.

Caines, Jeanette. *Abby.* Steven Kellogg, ill. Harper, 1973.

*Lapsley, Susan. *I Am Adopted.* Michael Charlton, ill. Bradbury, 1974.

Stein, Sara Bonnett. *The Adopted One.* Erika Stone, photo. Walker, 1979.

*Wasson, Valentina. *The Chosen Baby.* Glo Coalson, ill. Lippincott, 1977 revised.

Books About Disabilities
Orthopedic Impairments

Fanshawe, Elizabeth. *Rachel.* Bradbury, 1977.

*Fassler, Joan. *Howie Helps Himself.* Joe Lasker, ill. Whitman, 1975.

Greenfield, Eloise. *Darlene.* George Ford, ill. Methuen, 1980.

Mack, Nancy. *Tracy.* Heinz Kluetmeir, ill. Raintree, 1976.

*Stein, Sara Bonnett. *About Handicaps.* Dick Frank, photo. Walker, 1974.

*White, Paul. *Janet at School.* Crowell, 1978.

Wolf, Bernard. *Don't Feel Sorry for Paul.* Lippincott, 1974.

Visual Impairments

*Heide, Florence Parry. *Sound of Sunshine, Sound of Rain.* Kenneth Longtemps, ill. Four Winds, 1970.

*Litchfield, Ada. *A Cane in Her Hand.* Eleanor Mill, ill. Whitman, 1977.

*Petersen, Palle. *Sally Can't See.* Crowell-Day, 1977.

Wolf, Bernard. *Connie's New Eyes.* Lippincott, 1976.

Hearing Impairments

Charlip, Remy and MaryBeth. *Handtalk: An ABC of Finger Spelling.* George Ancona, photo. Four Winds, 1974.

Levine, Eda. *Lisa and Her Soundless World.* Gloria Kamen, ill. Human Science Press, 1973.

*Litchfield, Ada. *A Button in Her Ear.* Eleanor Mill, ill. Whitman, 1975.

*Peter, Diana. *Claire and Emma.* Jeremy Findlay, photo. Crowell-Day, 1977.

*Peterson, Jeanne Whitehouse. *I Have a Sister, My Sister Is Deaf.* Deborah Ray, ill. Harper, 1977.

*Wolf, Bernard. *Anna's Silent World.* Lippincott, 1977.

Slow Learners

*Brightman, Alan. *Like Me.* Little Brown, 1976.

Clifton, Lucille. *My Friend Jacob.* Dutton, 1980.

*Kraus, Robert. *Leo the Late Bloomer.* Jose Aruego, ill. Windmill/Simon & Schuster, 1971.

*Larsen, Hanne. *Don't Forget Tom.* Crowell, 1978.

*Lasker, Joe. *He's My Brother.* Whitman, 1974.

*Sobol, Harriet. *My Brother Steven Is Retarded.* Patricia Agre, photo. Macmillan, 1977.

Books With Varied Artistic Styles

*Chaucer, Geoffrey. *Chanticleer and the Fox.* Barbara Cooney, ill. and ad. Crowell, 1958.

*Emberley, Barbara, ad. *Drummer Hoff.* Ed Emberley, ill. Prentice-Hall, 1967.

*Ionesco, Eugene. *Story Number 1,* Etienne Delessert, ill. Harlan Quist, 1970.

*———*Story Number 2.* Etienne Delessert, ill. Harlan Quist, 1976.

*Keats, Ezra Jack. *Jennie's Hat.* Harper, 1966.

*———*The Snowy Day.* Viking, 1962.

*Lamorisse, Albert. *The Red Balloon.* Doubleday, 1956.

*Lionni, Leo. *Inch by Inch.* Obolensky, 1960.

*———*Swimmy.* Pantheon, 1960.

*McCloskey, Robert. *Make Way for Ducklings.* Viking, 1941.

*Piatti, Celestino. *The Happy Owls.* Atheneum, 1964.

*Potter, Beatrix. *The Tale of Peter Rabbit.* Warne, 1902.

*Prokofiev, Serge. *Peter and the Wolf.* Frans Haachen, ill. Watts, 1961.

*Sasek, Miroslav. *This Is Paris.* Macmillan, 1959.

*Ward, Lynd. *The Biggest Bear.* Houghton Mifflin, 1952.

Concept Books
ABC Books

*Anno, Mitsumasa. *Anno's Alphabet Book: An Adventure in Imagination.* Crowell, 1975.

Beisner, Monica. *A Folding Alphabet Book.* Farrar, 1981.

*Emberley, Ed. *Ed Emberley's ABC.* Little Brown, 1978.

Hyman, Trina Schart. *A Little Alphabet.* Little Brown, 1981.

*Lobel, Arnold. *On Market Street.* Anita Lobel, ill. Greenwillow, 1981.

McMillan, Bruce. *The Alphabet Symphony*. Greenwillow, 1977.

Milgrom, Harry. *ABC of Ecology*. Donald Crews, photo. Macmillan, 1972.

Musgrove, Margaret. *Ashanti to Zulu*. Leo and Diane Dillon, ill. Dial, 1976.

Provensen, Alice and Martin. *A Peaceable Kingdom: The Shaker Abecedarius*. Viking, 1978.

Rockwell, Anne. *Albert B. Cub and Zebra: An Alphabet Storybook*. Crowell, 1977.

*Schmiderer, Dorothy. *The Alphabeast Book: An Abecedarium*. Holt, 1971.

Tobias, Hosea and Lisa Baskin. *Hosie's Alphabet*. Leonard Baskin, ill. Viking, 1972.

Number Books

*Anno, Mitsumasa. *Anno's Counting Book*. Crowell, 1975.

*Bayley, Nicola. *One Old Oxford Ox*. Atheneum, 1978.

*Bruna, Dick. *I Can Count More*. Methuen, 1968.

*———*I Know More About Numbers*. Methuen, 1981.

Munari, Bruno. *Bruno Munari's Zoo*. Philomel, 1963.

Color Books

Chermayeff, Ivan. *Tomato and Other Colors*. Prentice-Hall, 1981.

*Emberley, Ed. *Green Says Go*. Little Brown, 1968.

Hirsch, Marilyn, ad. and ill. *How the World Got Its Color*. Crown, 1972.

*Lionni, Leo. *Little Blue and Little Yellow*. Obolensky, 1959.

———*A Color of His Own*. Pantheon, 1975.

Tison, Annette and Talus Taylor. *Adventures of the Three Colors*. Merrill, 1979.

*Zolotow, Charlotte. *Mr. Rabbit and the Lovely Present*. Maurice Sendak, ill. Harper, 1962.

Other Concept Books

*Carle, Eric. *The Secret Birthday Message*. Crowell, 1981 revised.

*Gardner, Beau. *The Turn About, Think About, Look About Book*. Greenwillow, 1980.

*Hoban, Tana. *Big Ones, Little Ones*. Greenwillow, 1976.

*———*Over, Under, and Through and Other Spatial Concepts*. Macmillan, 1973.

*———*Push Pull, Empty Full: A Book of Opposites*. Macmillan, 1972.

———*More Than One*. Greenwillow, 1981.

Schlein, Miriam. *Fast Is Not a Ladybug*. Leonard Kessler, ill. Addison-Wesley, 1953.

———*Heavy Is a Hippopotamus*. Leonard Kessler, ill. Addison-Wesley, 1954.

———*Shapes*. Sam Berman, ill. Addison-Wesley, 1952.

Spier, Peter. *Fast-Slow, High-Low*. Doubleday, 1972.

*Wildsmith, Brian. *What the Moon Saw*. Oxford University Press, 1978.

CHAPTER 6
AGES FIVE TO SIX

Know you what it is to be a child? . . . It is to have a spirit yet streaming from the water
of baptism; it is to believe in love, to believe in loveliness, to believe in belief;
it is to be so little that the elves can reach to whisper in your ear; it is to turn pumpkins into
coaches, and mice into horses, lowness into loftiness, and nothing into everything,
for each child has a fairy godmother in its soul.
—Frances Thompson
"Shelby"
The Dublin Review, 1908

Five is an exciting age. No longer nurseryschoolers, five-year-olds have an insatiable desire to learn about everything; they love to listen, to observe, to mimic, and to talk. And, although they are eager to enter the "real, grown-up" world, five-year-olds still love to pretend. Fortunately, they still retain the magical ability to enter the land of make-believe. A five-year-old's imaginative powers, increased attention span, developing sight vocabulary, and eagerness to read call for "word" books, beginning readers, poetry, picture stories with strong characters and plots, and more elaborate fantasy.

"WORD" BOOKS

Aware of the special relationship between the printed word and the spoken word, your child will now enjoy looking at books with large, printed words. All of the previously mentioned books that include labeled pictures like *Brian Wildsmith's ABC, Baby's First Book, Apples to Zippers: An Alphabet Book,* and *Let's Play* are appropriate now, so don't be too hasty as you clear off your child's bookshelf. Other suitable "word" books include Eric Carle's *My Very First Book of Words,* in which your child is challenged to find the word on the bottom half of the split page that matches the picture on the top half, and Dick Bruna's *I Can Read* and *I Can Read More. I Feel: A Picturebook of Emotions* by George Ancona is also popular with kindergarteners. In this large format book, black and white photographs show children displaying various emotions such as happiness, shyness, jealousy, and love. Accompanying each picture is a large, bold-faced word (in lower-case letters) to describe each emotion. Obviously, this book promotes word recognition, and it also promotes story-telling and emotion-sharing.

Five-year-olds also enjoy books *about* words—books that play with words and show all the wonderful things they can do. The word play books of Dr. Seuss and Fred Gwynne mentioned in Chapter 5 are excellent choices now as is Edith Baer's *Words Are Like Faces,* which celebrates in a rhyming text the many uses and characteristics of words: "Words can be plain/like a loaf of fresh bread,/comforting words/like your very own bed,/sheltering words/like the room where you play—/safe, snug and cozy,/and easy to say./Words can be/ fleet things,/light as a cloud,/lovely to hear/as you say them aloud—/sunlight and rain-bow,/snowflake and star—/they glimmer and shimmer and shine from afar."

Riddle books are also popular; favorites include Cynthia Basil's *Nailheads and Potato Eyes*, Polly Cameron's *The Two-Ton Canary and Other Nonsense Riddles,* and Riana Ducan's collection of traditional animal riddles *A Nutcracker in a Tree.*

I-CAN-READ BOOKS

If children have been exposed to the magic of books and to the joys that their texts and pictures have to offer, by five some will naturally be eager to read on their own. Encouraged by this desire and an increasing attention span, your child may be ready now for easy-to-read books. These specially designed books are characterized by interesting plots, lively characters, simple vocabulary, short sentences, and engaging pictures. Among the best are Harper and Row's I-Can-Read books. "Without using condescending language, or the hail-like patter of the first books in many reading series, these simply written stories," praises Constantine Georgiou in *Children and Their Literature,* "are made appealing and manageable by the simplicity and originality of their easy-to-read text. Wisely chosen words are used with imaginative pictures that offer clever clues to readers who may be doing their first independent reading. Many of the books in this series have the added convenience of being set in eighteen-point type, which is large and well-spaced enough to allow for easy reading."

One such book is Laura Jean Allen's *Ottie and the Star.* Intrigued by a star's shimmering reflections in the sea, Ottie the otter swims down deeper and deeper in search of one. After meeting a kind dolphin and a not-so-kind shark, Ottie finally does find a star—only to discover that it is a starfish! The hazy watercolor pictures and Ottie's innocent mistake make this I-Can-Read book a favorite.

Also popular is Crosby Bonsall's *Who's Afraid of the Dark?* in which a little boy confides to an older friend that his dog, Stella, is afraid of the dark: "When we go to bed she shivers. In the dark she shakes. She sees big scary shapes. She hears little scary sounds. She hears oooohs and booooos. I tell her it's only the wind. But Stella is still scared." It isn't long before the friend (and readers) realize that the dog is not the frightened one!

In Marjorie Weinman Sharmat's *Scarlet Monster Lives Here,* another Harper I-Can-Read book that is sure to promote both laughter and reading skills, Scarlet is so busy decorating her new house, baking brownies, pickling beets, and painting welcome signs that she almost misses the neighbors who are shyly waiting to welcome her to the neighborhood. At first, when no one visits her, the worried Scarlet sadly concludes that no one likes her because she is a monster who weighs 300 lbs. and has crooked fangs, but a delightful surprise awaits both Scarlet and young readers.

Other I-Can-Read favorites include Else Holmelund Minarik's *Little Bear* series and Arnold Lobel's celebration of friendship, the *Frog and Toad* series. Other excellent easy-to-read books are the Little Owl books published by Holt, Rinehart & Winston, Random House's I Can Read It By Myself Beginning Books, and Dial's Easy-to-Read books.

POETRY

Since your child is just beginning a love affair with words that will last a lifetime, now is an appropriate time to introduce more poetry. Literary critic Northrop Frye says that "poetry is the most direct and simple means of expressing oneself in words.... Poetry is not irregular lines in a book, but something very close to dance and song, something to walk down the street keeping in time to."

Kindergarteners, like younger children, naturally respond to the music of poetry; they like its meter, its rhyme, its imagery. They like to hear it, and they like to say it. If poetry brings back painful memories of standing before a class reciting lengthy stanzas, please give poetry another chance. Explore some of the poetry books available for children today, and help your child to recognize poetry as a friend rather than a dreaded enemy. The world of poetry is a rich and varied one, from classic masters like William Shakespeare and William Blake to contemporary wordsmiths like Eve Merriam and Eloise Greenfield. Help your child feel comfortable in this fascinating world.

Children's poetry is not only about children, woodland creatures, and flowers. From monsters to horses, from gnomes to trains, there is poetry on just about any imaginative topic. Have fun and enjoy the poems that you will meet along the way as you search for your child's favorite subjects.

"When I'm by myself/And I close my eyes/I'm a twin/I'm a dimple on a chin/I'm a roomful of toys…I'm a whatever I want to be/An anything I care to be/And when I open my eyes/What I care to be/Is me." This is just one of many "love" poems that my students loved in Eloise Greenfield's *Honey I Love and Other Love Poems*. Other favorite poetry books include *Monster Poems*, edited by Daisy Wallace, silly-scary poems highlighted by Kay Chorao's hilarious pictures; *In a Spring Garden*, edited by Richard Lewis, a collection of haiku illustrated by Ezra Jack Keats' collages celebrating a spring day from a snail's reaction to a vibrant red dawn to the twinkling goodnight of a giant firefly; and Edward Lear's classic *The Owl and the Pussycat*. The sing-song quality of this nonsense tale captures young listeners' attention, and best-loved editions include those illustrated by Gwen Fulton and Barbara Cooney.

PICTURE STORYBOOKS

Your five-year-old is also ready for stories with strong plots, more elaborate fantasy, developed characters, and detailed illustrations. Story picturebooks, which are a bit more sophisticated than simple picturebooks since they have more text, are ideal now. Favorites include Don Freeman's *Will's Quill*, the story of an adventurous country goose who befriends a young playwright named Will Shakespeare; Robert McCloskey's *Make Way for Ducklings*, the saga of a mallard duck family who relocates to Boston; and William Steig's *Amos and Boris*, the bittersweet tale of an unlikely pair, a mouse and a whale, who become best friends.

Stories about bears seem to hold a special place in the hearts of five-year-olds, and Winnie-the-Pooh, Corduroy, and Paddington are all well-loved storybook characters. Elephants, too, are popular as Jean DeBrunhoff's *Babar* books prove.

To supplement picture storybooks, now is also a good time to introduce your five-year-old to lengthy classics that can be shared a chapter at a time, depending on your child's attention span and interest. Laura Ingalls Wilder's *Little House* books and E.B. White's *Charlotte's Web* are appropriate choices as are L. Frank Baum's *The Wizard of Oz* and J.M. Barrie's *Peter Pan*. One exceptionally fine version of Barrie's fanciful adventure of the three Darling children and the boy who didn't want to grow up is Trina Schart Hyman's beautifully illustrated gift edition.

An excellent way to introduce your child to Kenneth Grahame's *The Wind in the Willows* is with Scribner's *The River Bank*, *The Open Road*, and *Wayfarers All*, which immortalize selected chapters about Toad, Mole, and Rat in beautifully illustrated picturebook form.

FABLES, FOLK TALES, AND FAIRY TALES

Longer attention spans and the growing ability to distinguish between fantasy and reality make fables, folk tales, and fairy tales popular with five-year-olds. Although fables were not originally written for children, they enjoy the moralizing animal tales of Aesop because they are brief, simple, and deal with universal themes that are easy to identify with. Outstanding editions include Eve Rice's *Once in a Wood: Ten Tales from Aesop* and those illustrated by Randolph Caldecott, Eric Carle, and Paul Galdone.

La Fontaine is also a favorite. Look for Brian Wildsmith's colorful versions of *The Hare and the Tortoise, The Miller, the Boy, and the Donkey,* and *The North Wind and the Sun.*

Single-fable books like Marcia Brown's *Once a Mouse* and Paul Galdone's *The Monkeys and the Crocodile* are especially appropriate for five-year-olds.

Right next to Aesop and La Fontaine, make room on your child's bookshelf for Arnold Lobel's *Fables.* This large-format picturebook stars a ballet-dancing camel and a love-struck ostrich. Complemented by pastel-colored illustrations, each original fable satirizes common human follies such as pride, complacency, vanity, and greed.

Since five-year-olds usually have a distinct curiosity about other peoples and cultures, folk tales from other countries are appealing. Favorites include Gail Haley's *A Story, A Story,* an African tale highlighted by vivid woodcuts; *Tikki Tikki Tempo,* a Chinese tale retold by Arlene Mosel; and Verna Aardema's *Why Mosquitoes Buzz in People's Ears,* a Masai tale illustrated by Leo and Diane Dillon's watercolor and pastel pictures. Also popular are Gerald McDermott's *Anansi the Spider: A Tale from the Ashanti, The Stonecutter: A Japanese Folk Tale,* and *Arrow to the Sun: A Pueblo Indian Tale,* each brilliantly enhanced by dramatic, stylized illustrations.

The average five-year-old is ready for simple fairy tales. Your child will probably delight in hearing about wicked witches, giants, cruel punishments, and the threat of wolves and ogres, knowing that he or she is safe and secure by your side. But since children differ in impressionability and susceptibility, remember that you are the best judge as to which fairy tales are appropriate for your child. It's wise to begin with the gentler, simpler stories and then progress gradually to the others after you screen them for frightening elements.

The controversy over the suitability of fairy tales for children is almost as old as the tales themselves. Countless critics, among them Sarah Trimmer who in 1806 branded Cinderella as "a monster of deceit" and accused this Perrault story of "some of the worst passions that can enter into the human breast, and of which little children should, if possible, be totally ignorant, such as envy, jealousy, a dislike of mothers-in-law, half sisters, vanity, a love of dress, etc., etc.," have censored fairy tales for their gory details and condemned them as vehicles of escapism for children who prefer to retreat into a world of fantasy instead of facing the real world. However, proponents of the tales, including C.S. Lewis, Kornei Chukovsky, J.R.R. Tolkien, and Bruno Bettelheim, contend that the tales not only cultivate children's imaginations, pave the way for an appreciation of literature, and expose children to different cultures, but they are also therapeutic, conveying moral guidance without sermonizing and satisfying children's needs for self-expression and their need to confront anxieties and wishes. Rather than providing a means of escape, fairy tales actually help children understand themselves and their complex world and provide a way for children to deal with strong emotions in a safe way. "Each fairy tale," states child psychologist Bruno Bettelheim in *The Uses of Enchantment: The Meaning and Importance of Fairy Tales,* "is a magic mirror which reflects some aspect of our inner world, and of the steps required by our evolution from immaturity to maturity."

Fairy tales hold a special magic for children and for adults. Commonly called household

tales (and they *do* belong in every household), stories about elves, fairies, wizards, the poor who become rich, and silly folk possess all the elements that appeal to children. They imaginatively deal with universal themes such as love, greed, beauty, courage, and vanity. Fairy tales are full of action; their plots are suspenseful and based on trials, quests, and conflicts between good and evil—Jack against the Giant, Hansel and Gretel against the witch. Fairy tale characters are easily understood by children; they are not real people but types who are ultimately either punished or rewarded. The moral questions in fairy tales are black and white, which especially satisfies children who are not yet aware of the subtle shades of gray.

There are numerous fairy tale collections available; use the same criteria for evaluation that you used to select a Mother Goose collection (Chapter 1).

Especially fine fairy tale anthologies include *Grimm's Fairy Tales*, stories including *Snowdrop* and *Rumpelstiltskin*, illustrated by Arthur Rackham's eerie pictures and silhouettes; *Perrault's Complete Fairy Tales*, including *Little Red Riding Hood* and *Beauty and the Beast*, illustrated by W. Heath Robinson's black and white sketches; *Fairy Tales*, Perrault and Grimm favorites including *Tom Thumb* and *The Babes in the Wood*, illustrated by Margaret Tarrant; and *Ardizzone's Hans Anderson*, tales including *Thumbelina* and *The Ugly Duckling*, illustrated by color and black and white Ardizzone pictures. You should also look at Dover's edition of *Perrault's Fairy Tales*, but I feel that Gustave Doré's illustrations are much too frightening for young children.

Perfectly suited to your five-year-old's tiny hands, *Fairy Tale Library* is a collection of six favorites: *Snow White, Hansel and Gretel, Jack and the Beanstalk, Puss-in-Boots, Sleeping Beauty,* and *Cinderella*. Each miniature volume is illustrated by Jan Pienkowski's striking silhouettes and full-color pictures. Beautifully designed with marbleized endpapers and hand lettering, this collection recaptures the charm of the Victorian era.

Single-tale picturebooks are especially suitable for young children because they make each tale special to a child. As one of my young students put it, "Each story has a whole book of its own." Favorites include Susan Jeffers' lovely interpretations of *Thumbelina, Snow White and the Seven Dwarfs,* and *Hansel and Gretel*. Each of these large-format books is dominated by Jeffers' glowing pictures, which simply have to be seen to be fully appreciated.

Other favorites include Nonny Hogrogian's *Cinderella*, which is softly illustrated with colored pencils, and Trina Schart Hyman's *Snow White*, which has an eerie, dark, mysterious quality that my students loved as much as Jeffers' pastel-dominated illustrations.

After reading a fairy tale, I always show my students several illustrated versions. They (and I) never tire of looking at and comparing each illustrator's visual interpretation of these "happily ever after" tales.

BOOKS FOR FIVE-YEAR-OLDS

Use this list together with all the previous lists. For easy reference, books are grouped thematically and alphabetized by author. Those mentioned in this chapter are marked with an asterisk (*).

"Word" Books

*Ancona, George. *I Feel: A Picturebook of Emotions.* Dutton, 1977.

*Baer, Edith. *Words Are Like Faces.* Karen Gundersheimer, ill. Pantheon, 1980.

*Basil, Cynthia. *Nailheads and Potato Eyes.* Janet McCaffery, ill. Morrow, 1976.

Bester, Roger. *Guess What?* Crown, 1981.

Bracken, Carolyn. *Animal Crackers: A Menagerie of Jokes and Riddles.* Platt & Munk, 1979.

*Bruna, Dick. *I Can Read.* Methuen, 1965.

*———*I Can Read More.* Methuen, 1968.

*Cameron, Polly. *The Two-Ton Canary and Other Nonsense Riddles.* Coward, 1978.

*Carle, Eric. *My Very First Book of Words.* Crowell, 1974.

DeRegniers, Beatrice S. *It Does Not Say Meow.* Paul Galdone, ill. Houghton Mifflin, 1972.

*Ducan, Riana. *A Nutcracker in a Tree: A Book of Riddles.* Delacorte, 1980.

Rothman, Joel and Argentina Palacios. *This Can Lick a Lollipop: Body Riddles for Kids.* Doubleday, 1979.

Beginning Readers

*Allen, Laura Jean. *Ottie and the Star.* Harper, 1979.

Baker, Betty. *Rat Is Dead and Ant Is Sad.* Mamoru Funai, ill. Harper, 1981.

*Bonsall, Crosby. *Who's Afraid of the Dark?* Harper, 1980.

———*The Case of the Double Cross.* Harper. 1980.

Bram, Elizabeth. *Woodruff and the Clocks.* Dial, 1980.

Bulla, Clyde Robert. *Daniel's Duck.* Joan Sandin, ill. Harper, 1979.

Chorao, Kay. *Oink and Pearl.* Harper, 1981.

Coerr, Eleanor. *The Big Balloon Race.* Carolyn Croll, ill. Harper, 1981.

Hoban, Lillian. *Arthur's Funny Money.* Harper, 1981.

———*Mr. Pig and Family.* Harper, 1980.

Kwitz, Mary DeBall. *Little Chick's Big Day.* Bruce Degen, ill. Harper, 1981.

Lewis, Thomas P. *Call for Mr. Sniff.* Beth Weiner Woldin, ill. Harper, 1981.

*Lobel, Arnold. *Frog and Toad Together.* Harper, 1971.

*———*Frog and Toad Are Friends.* Harper, 1970.

———*Mouse Soup.* Harper, 1977.

———*Owl at Home.* Harper, 1975.

———*Small Pig.* Harper, 1969.

———*Uncle Elephant.* Harper, 1981.

Manushkin, Fran. *The Perfect Christmas Picture.* Karen Ann Weinhaus, ill. Harper, 1979.

Marshall, James. *Troll Country.* Dial, 1980.

*Minarik, Else Holmelund. *Little Bear.* Maurice Sendak, ill. Harper, 1957.

*———*Father Bear Comes Home.* Maurice Sendak, ill. Harper, 1959.

*———*Little Bear's Friend.* Maurice Sendak, ill. Harper, 1960.

*———*Little Bear's Visit.* Maurice Sendak, ill. Harper, 1961.

*———*A Kiss for Little Bear.* Maurice Sendak, ill. Harper, 1968.

Parish, Peggy. *No More Monsters for Me!* Marc Simont, ill. Harper, 1981.

Pearson, Susan. *Molly Moves Out.* Steven Kellogg, ill. Dial, 1979.

Schick, Eleanor. *Home Alone.* Dial, 1980.

*Sharmat, Marjorie Weinman. *Scarlet Monster Lives Here.* Dennis Kendrick, ill. Harper, 1979.

Shecter, Ben. *Hester the Jester.* Harper, 1978.

Wittman, Sally. *Plenty of Pelly and Peak.* Harper, 1981.

Van Leeuwen, Jean. *Tales of Oliver Pig.* Arnold Lobel, ill. Dial, 1979.

———*More Tales of Oliver Pig.* Arnold Lobel, ill. Dial, 1981.

Poetry

Agree, Rose. *How To Eat a Poem and Other Morsels: A Collection of Food Poems for Children.* Peggy Wilson, ill. Random House, 1967.

Arbuthnot, May Hill and Shelton L. Root, Jr., eds. *Time for Poetry,* third edition. Arthur Paul, ill. Scott, Foresman, 1968.

Ciardi, John. *I Met a Man.* Robert Osborn, ill. Houghton Mifflin, 1961.

———*You Read to Me, I'll Read to You.* Edward Gorey, ill. Lippincott, 1981.

Cole, William. *Poem Stew.* Karen Weinhaus, ill. Lippincott, 1981.

Fields, Eugene. *Wynken, Blynken, and Nod.* Barbara Cooney, ill. Hastings House, 1981 (reissue).

Fisher, Aileen. *Anybody Home?* Susan Bonners, ill. Crowell, 1980.

Frost, Robert. *Stopping By Woods on a Snowy Evening.* Susan Jeffers, ill. Dutton, 1978.

*Greenfield, Eloise. *Honey I Love and Other Love Poems.* Leo and Diane Dillon, ill. Crowell, 1978.

Hopkins, Lee Bennett, ed. *By Myself.* Glo Coalson, ill. Crowell, 1980.

———*Elves, Fairies, and Gnomes.* Rosekrans Hoffman, ill. Knopf, 1980.

Klagsbrum, Francine, ed. *Free to Be You and Me.* McGraw, 1974.

Larrick, Nancy, ed. *Piping Down the Valleys Wild.* Ellen Raskin, ill. Delacorte, 1968.

*Lear, Edward. *The Owl and the Pussycat.* Gwen Fulton, ill. Atheneum, 1978.

*———*Le Hibou et La Poussiquette (The Owl and the Pussycat).* Francis Steegmueler, trans. Barbara Cooney, ill. Little Brown, 1961.

*Lewis, Richard, ed. *In a Spring Garden.* Ezra Jack Keats, ill. Dial, 1965.

Livingston, Myra Cohen, ed. *Listen, Children, Listen.* Trina Schart Hyman, ill. Harcourt, 1972.

Merriam, Eve. *There Is No Rhyme for Silver.* Joseph Schindelman, ill. Atheneum, 1962.

———*Catch a Little Rhyme.* Imero Gobbato, ill. Atheneum, 1966.

Milne, A.A. *Now We Are Six.* Ernest Shephard, ill. Dutton, 1927.

———*When We Were Very Young.* Ernest Shephard, ill. Dutton, 1924.

Prelutsky, Jack. *The Headless Horseman Rides Again.* Arnold Lobel, ill. Greenwillow, 1980.

Sendak, Maurice. *Chicken Soup with Rice (Nutshell Library).* Harper, 1962.

Stevenson, Robert Louis. *A Child's Garden of Verses.* Jessie Wilcox Smith, ill. Scribner, 1905, 1969.

———*A Child's Garden of Verses.* Charles Robinson, ill. Green Tiger Press, 1976.

*Wallace, Daisy, ed. *Monster Poems.* Kay Chorao, ill. Holiday House, 1976.

———ed. *Fairy Poems.* Trina Schart Hyman, ill. Holiday House, 1980.

———ed. *Ghost Poems.* Tomie De Paola, ill. Holiday House, 1979.

———ed. *Giant Poems.* Margot Tomes, ill. Holiday House, 1978.

———ed. *Witch Poems.* Trina Schart Hyman, ill. Holiday House, 1976.

Zolotow, Charlotte. *River Winding.* Zazue Mizumura, ill. Crowell, 1978.

Picture Storybooks

*Barrie, J.M. *Peter Pan.* Trina Schart Hyman, ill. Scribner, 1980.

*Baum, Frank L. *The Wizard of Oz.* W.W. Denslow, ill. Macmillan, 1970.

*Bond, Michael. *A Bear Called Paddington.* Houghton Mifflin, 1960.

Cleaver, Elizabeth. *Petrouchka.* Atheneum, 1980.

Cunningham, Julian. *A Mouse Called Junction.* Michael Hague, ill. Pantheon, 1980.

Daly, Niki. *Vim the Rag Mouse,* Atheneum, 1979.

*De Brunhoff. *The Story of Babar.* Random House, 1937.

Flack, Marjorie. *The Story of Ping.* Kurt Wiese, ill. Viking, 1933.

*Freeman, Don. *Will's Quill.* Viking Press, 1975.

*Grahame, Kenneth. *The Open Road.* Beverley Gooding, ill. Scribner, 1980.

*———*Wayfarers All.* Beverley Gooding, ill. Scribner, 1981.

*———*The River Bank.* Adrienne Adams, ill. Scribner, 1979.

Haas, Irene. *The Little Moon Theater.* Atheneum, 1981.

Hale, Irina. *Chocolate Mouse and Sugar Pig and How They Ran Away to Escape Being Eaten.* Atheneum, 1981.

Hall, Donald. *The Ox-Cart Man.* Barbara Cooney, ill. Viking, 1979.

Hoffman, E.T.A. *The Nutcracker.* Janet Schulman, ad. Kay Chorao, ill. Dutton, 1979.

Jacques, Faith. *Tilly's House.* Atheneum, 1979.

———*Tilly's Rescue.* Atheneum, 1981.

*McCloskey, Robert. *Make Way for Ducklings.* Viking, 1941.

*Milne, A.A. *The House at Pooh Corner.* Ernest Shephard, ill. Dutton, 1928.

———*Winnie-the-Pooh.* Ernest Shephard, ill. Dutton, 1926.

———*The World of Pooh.* Ernest Shephard, ill. Dutton, 1957.

Sharmat, Marjorie Weinman. *I'm Terrific.* Kay Chorao, ill. Holiday House, 1977.

———*Grumley the Grouch.* Kay Chorao, ill. Holiday House, 1980.

———*Mr. Jameson and Mr. Phillips.* Bruce Degen, ill. Harper, 1979.

———*Taking Care of Melvin.* Victoria Chess, ill. Holiday House, 1980.

—— *Thornton the Worrier.* Kay Chorao, ill. Holiday House, 1978.

—— *Twitchell the Wishful.* Janet Stevens, ill. Holiday House, 1981.

*Steig, William. *Amos and Boris.* Farrar, 1971.

—— *Sylvester and the Magic Pebble.* Simon & Schuster, 1969.

*White, E.B. *Charlotte's Web.* Garth Williams, ill. Harper, 1952.

*Wilder, Laura Ingalls. *The Little House Books.* Garth Williams, ill. Harper, 1953.

Williams, Margery. *The Velveteen Rabbit.* William Nocolson, ill. Doubleday, 1958.

Fables, Folk Tales, and Fairy Tales

Aardema, Verna. *Who's in Rabbit's House?* Diane and Leo Dillon, ill. Dial, 1977.

*—— *Why Mosquitoes Buzz in People's Ears.* Diane and Leo Dillon, ill. Dial, 1975.

Aesop. *Aesop's Fables.* Heidi Holder, ill. Viking, 1981.

*—— *The Caldecott Aesop.* Randolph Caldecott, ill. Doubleday, 1978.

*—— *The Hare and the Tortoise.* Paul Galdone, ill. McGraw, 1962.

*—— *Once in a Wood: Ten Tales from Aesop.* Eve Rice, ad. and ill. Greenwillow, 1979.

*—— *Three Aesop Fox Fables.* Paul Galdone, ill. Houghton Mifflin, 1971.

*—— *Twelve Tales from Aesop.* Eric Carle, ill. Philomel, 1980.

*Anderson, Hans Christian. *Ardizzone's Hans Anderson.* Stephen Corrin, trans. Edward Ardizzone, ill. Atheneum, 1979.

—— *Michael Hague's Favorite Hans Christian Anderson Fairy Tales.* Michael Hague, ill. Holt, 1981.

—— *The Snow Queen.* Naomi Lewis, ad. Errol Le Cain, ill. Viking, 1979.

—— *Thumbeline.* Richard and Clara Winston, trans. Lisbeth Zwerger, ill. Greenwillow, 1980.

Berends, Polly Berrien, ad. *Jack Kent's Nursery Tales.* Jack Kent, ill. Random House, 1970.

*Brown, Marcia, ad. and ill. *Once a Mouse.* Scribner, 1962.

—— ad. and ill. *Stone Soup.* Scribner, 1947.

—— ad. and ill. *The Three Billy Goats Gruff.* Harcourt, 1957.

*Chaucer, Geoffrey. *Chanticleer and the Fox.* Barbara Cooney, ill. Crowell, 1958.

Daugherty, James. *Andy and the Lion.* Viking, 1938.

De Paola, Tomie, ad. and ill. *The Legend of Old Befena.* Harcourt, 1981.

Dewey, Ariane, ad. and ill. *The Thunder God's Son.* Greenwillow, 1980.

*Ehrlich, Amy, reteller. *Thumbelina.* Susan Jeffers, ill. Dial, 1979.

—— *The Wild Swans.* Susan Jeffers, ill. Dial, 1981.

*Galdone, Paul, ad. and ill. *The Monkeys and the Crocodile.* Houghton Mifflin, 1969.

Goble, Paul, ad. and ill. *The Gift of the Sacred Dog.* Bradbury, 1981.

*Grimm, Jacob and Wilhelm. *Grimm's Fairy Tales.* Arthur Rackham, ill. Viking, 1973.

—— *Hansel and Gretel.* Elizabeth D. Crawford, trans. Lisbeth Zwerger, ill. Greenwillow, 1979.

*—— *Hansel and Gretel.* Susan Jeffers, ill. Dial, 1980.

———— *Rare Treasures from Grimm.* Ralph Manhiem, compiler. Erik Blegvad, ill. Doubleday, 1981.

———— *The Seven Ravens.* Elizabeth D. Crawford, trans. Lisbeth Zwerger, ill. Greenwillow, 1980.

———— *The Shoemaker and the Elves.* Wayne Andrews, trans. Adrianne Adams, ill. Atheneum, 1981.

*———— *Snow White.* Paul Heins, trans. Trina Schart Hyman, ill. Little Brown, 1974.

———— *Snow White and the Seven Dwarfs.* Randall Jarrell, trans. Nancy Ekholm Burket, ill. Farrar, 1972.

*———— *Snow White and the Seven Dwarfs.* Susan Jeffers, ill. Dial, 1980.

Hague, Michael and Kathleen, ad. *East of the Sun and West of the Moon.* Michael Hague, ill. Harcourt, 1981.

*Haley, Gail. *A Story, A Story.* Atheneum, 1970.

Haviland, Virginia, ed. *The Fairy Tale Treasury.* Raymond Briggs, ill. Coward, 1972.

*Hogrogian, Nonny, ad. and ill. *Cinderella.* Greenwillow, 1980.

*La Fontaine, Jean de. *The Hare and the Tortoise.* Brian Wildsmith, ill. Watts, 1967.

*———— *The Miller, the Boy, and the Donkey.* Brian Wildsmith, ill. Watts, 1969.

*———— *The North Wind and the Sun.* Brian Wildsmith, ill. Watts, 1964.

———— *The Rich Man and the Shoemaker.* Brian Wildsmith, ill. Oxford, 1980.

*Lobel, Arnold. *Fables.* Harper, 1980.

Lurie, Allison, ed. *Clever Gretchen and Other Forgotten Folktales.* Margot Tomes, ill. Crowell, 1980.

Mayer, Marianna, ad. *Beauty and the Beast.* Mercer Mayer, ill. Four Winds, 1978.

*McDermott, Gerald, *Anansi the Spider: A Tale from the Ashanti.* Holt, 1971.

*———— *Arrow to the Sun: A Pueblo Indian Tale.* Viking, 1977.

———— *The Magic Tree: A Tale from the Congo.* Holt, 1973.

*———— *The Stonecutter: A Japanese Folktale.* Viking, 1975.

*Mosel, Arlene. *Tikki Tikki Tempo.* Blair Lent, ill. Holt, 1968.

*Perrault, Charles. *Perrault's Complete Fairy Tales.* A.E. Johnson, trans. William Heath Robinson, ill. Dodd, 1961.

*———— *Perrault's Fairy Tales.* A.E. Johnson, trans. Gustave Doré, ill. Dover, 1969.

Provensen, Alice and Martin, compilers and ill. *The Provensen Book of Fairy Tales.* Random House, 1971.

Rojankovsky, Feodor, ill. *The Tall Book Of Nursery Tales.* Harper, 1944.

Rose, Anne, ad. *Akimba and the Magic Cow: A Folktale from Africa.* Hopi Meryman, ill. Four Winds, 1976.

*Tarrant, Margaret, ill. *Fairy Tales.* Crowell, 1978.

*Tudor, Tasha, ill. *The Tasha Tudor Book of Fairy Tales.* Platt & Munk, 1980.

*Walser, David, trans. and ad. *Fairy Tale Library.* Jan Pienkowski, ill. Crowell, 1978.

Wolkstein, Diane. *A Cool Ride in the Sky.* Paul Galdone, ill. Knopf, 1973.

Yolen, Jane. *The Sultan's Perfect Tree.* Barbara Garrison, ill. Four Winds, 1977.

Zemach, Harve, ad. *Duffy and the Devil: A Cornish Tale.* Margot Zemach, ill. Farrar, 1973.

CONCLUSION

Is the world all grown up? Is childhood dead? Or is there not in the bosom of the wisest and the best some of the child's heart left, to respond to earliest enchantments?
—Lamb

Your introductory tour is over, but your major excursion is just beginning. I hope you now feel more at home in the land of children's books. Unlike many, when one says, "children's books," you do not automatically think of the drugstore and five-and-dime variety. You realize that the field of children's literature is a fascinating, multifaceted one, one that has undergone dramatic changes over the years. You are not complacent; you do not settle. You are critical and selective, aware of the various types of books that are appropriate for your child at different developmental levels. Congratulations, and keep up the good work! As your child grows and as the field expands, you have a lot of happy work ahead of you. Here are some guidelines to help you sharpen your critical sense, deepen your appreciation of children's literature as a legitimate literary genre, give you a historical perspective of the field, and heighten your confidence as a "judge" of good children's books:

1. Read children's books—lots and lots of them. Read the award-winners and the award-losers. Remember that awards are intended to improve children's tastes not rubber-stamp their favorites. *Charlotte's Web* "lost" the Newberry Award in 1953, and it has sold over 10,000 copies annually since its publication 29 years ago! And Laura Ingalls Wilder's Little House books were Newberry runners-up for five years, and we all know how loved these books are.

2. Make the children's room of your local library a familiar place. Take notice of which books are circulation-worn and which are being read at the library. Don't be intimidated by the misconception that libraries are quiet, stuffy places. Most good children's rooms have changed a great deal since you were straining to sign your first library card. Today you'll be delighted to find colorful posters and mobiles, an array of audio-visual equipment, and even a playpen in the children's room of the library. The atmosphere will invite you and your young child to feel welcomed; so browse often. Borrow books regularly and, if possible, buy special books that you feel should belong to your child.

3. Read books about children's books. Those listed in the bibliography are all appropriate. Also read book reviews about children's books in *The New York Times* (they devote special spring, fall, and holiday issues to children's books), *The Horn Book Magazine*, and "educator" magazines like *Teacher*, *Early Years*, and *Instructor*.

4. Talk to knowledgeable people in the field like teachers, librarians, critics, reviewers, writers, illustrators, and booksellers. Be open-minded but not gullible. Also, don't overlook

"nonprofessionals" who love children and their books; talk to other parents and share ideas with them.

5. Take a college course in children's literature. My classes in children's literature have always been a pleasant mixture of education majors, teachers, and parents, and even grandparents, all with one thing in common—a genuine interest in children and their books. Most schools offer classes for credit, and many allow students to simply audit. Call or write to the education or English department of your local college for more information.

6. Familiarize yourself with the many book selection aids that are available. Here is a *very* select listing:

*The American Library Association, 50 E. Huron Street, Chicago, IL 60611, publishes several useful lists including "Notable Children's Books of the Year."

*"Bibliography of Books for Children" is available from the Association for Childhood Education International, 3615 Wisconsin Avenue, N.W., Washington, DC 20016.

*The Book Stork, my mail-order children's book selection and consultation service offers any children's book in print at 10 percent off publishers' prices. An annotated brochure is available for $2.00; lists on requested special topic books are 50¢ each. Write to: The Book Stork, 44 Tee-Ar Place, Princeton, NJ 08540.

*"Bulletin of the Center for Children's Books" is published by the Graduate Library School of The University of Chicago.

*The Children's Book Council, 67 Irving Place, New York, NY 10003, is a clearinghouse for information on children's literature. Its reading rooms are open Monday through Friday, and it offers a wide array of Children's Book Week paraphernalia including posters, bookmarks, friezes, mobiles, and cassettes. In addition, the Council offers sheets and pamphlets on a wide variety of topics: "Choosing a Child's Book," "Writing Children's Books," "Illustrating Children's Books," "Newberry and Caldecott Medals," and "Children's Choices" (together with ALA and the International Reading Association). A materials brochure is available as is *The Calendar,* the official newsletter of the Council. Single copies of most items are free; there is a $5.00 one-time-only handling charge to place your name on the Council's mailing list.

The Horn Book Magazine is a bimonthly publication that includes critical articles and reviews. Write to: The Horn Book, Inc., Park Square Bldg. 31 St. James Avenue, Boston, MA 02116, for subscription information and for information about "Why Children's Books," their parent newsletter.

*"The Kirkus Review" is a bimonthly publication available at your library.

*"School Library Journal" is a monthly review publication available at your library.

As you select books for your children, keep in mind that your primary goal should be not only to get books into their hands, but into their minds and hearts as well. Share your enthusiasm, your spirit, your appreciation, and your love for books—it will be contagious. And your journey into the land of children's books will be an enjoyable adventure into a fascinating world—a world, which, even as an adult, you never need outgrow. Remember what W. H. Auden said about *Alice's Adventures in Wonderland,* "There are good books which are only for adults because their comprehension presupposes adult experiences, but there are no good books which are only for children." Bon voyage and happy reading!

BIBLIOGRAPHY OF BOOKS FOR ADULTS

While enjoying the pleasures to be found in books written especially for children, also explore some "grown-up" books. The following is a sampling of outstanding titles on children's literature and child development just waiting to be read.

Anderson, Verna. *Reading and Young Children.* Macmillan, 1968.

The Annotated Mother Goose, with introduction and notes by William Baring-Gould and Cecil Baring-Gould, ill. by Caldecott, Crane, Greenaway, Rackham, Parrish, and historical woodcuts. Potter, 1962.

Arbuthnot, May Hill. *Children and Books,* sixth edition. Scott, Foresman, 1980.

———*Children's Reading the Home.* Scott, Foresman, 1969.

Arbuthnot, May Hill and Zena Sutherland. *The Arbuthnot Anthology,* fourth edition. Scott, Foresman, 1976.

Bader, Barbara. *American Picturebooks from Noah's Ark to the Beast Within.* Macmillan, 1976.

Barata-Lorton, Mary. *Workjobs for Parents: Activity Centered Learning in the Home.* Addison-Wesley, 1975.

Baskin, Barbara and Karen Harris. *Notes From a Different Drummer: A Guide to Juvenile Fiction Portraying the Handicapped.* Bowker, 1977.

Baum, Frank. *The Annotated Wizard of Oz.* notes by Michael P. Hearn. Potter, 1973.

Bechtel, Louise Seaman, ed. *Books in Search of Children.* Macmillan, 1969.

Bettelheim, Bruno. *The Uses of Enchantment: Meaning and Importance of Fairy Tales.* Knopf, 1976.

Boston Women's Health Collective Inc. *Ourselves and Our Children: A Book by and for Parents.* Random House, 1978.

Braga, Laurie and Joseph. *Learning and Growing: A Guide to Child Development.* Prentice-Hall, 1975.

Butler, Dorothy. *Babies Need Books.* Atheneum, 1980.

———*Cushla and Her Books.* Horn Book, 1975.

Cameron, Eleanor. *The Green and Burning Tree: On Writing and Enjoyment of Children's Books.* Little, 1969.

Caplan, Frank, ed. *The First Twelve Months of Life: Your Baby's Growth Month by Month.* Grosset & Dunlap, 1973.

Caplan, Frank and Theresa, eds. *The Second Twelve Months of Life: Your Baby's Growth Month by Month.* Grosset & Dunlap, 1979.

Caplan, Frank and Theresa. *The Power of Play.* Doubleday, Anchor, 1973.

Carroll, Lewis (pseud.). *The Annotated Alice: Alice's Adventures in Wonderland and Through the Looking Glass.* ill. by John Tenniel, introduction and notes by Martin Gardner. Potter, 1960.

Chambers, Aidan. *Introducing Books to Children.* Horn Book, 1975.

Chukovsky, Kornei. *From Two to Five.* trans. and ed. by Miriam Morton. University of California Press, 1965.

Cianciolo, Patricia. *Illustrations in Children's Books,* second edition. Brown, 1976.

Cohen, Dorothy. *The Learning Child: Guidelines for Parents and Teachers.* Random House, 1972.

Colby, Jean Poindexter. *Writing, Illustrating and Editing Children's Books.* Hastings, 1967.

Commire, Anne. *Something About the Author: Facts and Pictures About Contemporary Authors and Illustrators of Books for Young People.* Vol. 1, Gale, 1971.

Coody, Betty. *Using Literature With Young Children.* Brown, 1973.

Doyle, Brian, comp. and ed. *The Who's Who of Children's Literature.* Schocken, 1969.

Egoff, Sheila, G.T. Stubbs, and L.F. Ashley, eds. *Only Connect: Readings on Children's Literature.* Oxford, 1969.

Erikson, Erik H. *Childhood and Society,* second edition. Norton, 1964.

Fassler, Joan. *Helping Children Cope: Mastering Stress Through Books and Stories.* Free Press, Macmillan, 1978.

Feaver, William. *When We Were Young: Two Centuries of Children's Book Illustration.* Holt, 1977.

Fraiberg, Selma. *The Magic Years: Understanding and Handling the Problems of Early Childhood.* Scribner, 1968.

Georgiou, Constantine. *Children and Their Literature.* Prentice-Hall, 1969.

Gersoni-Stavn, Diane, ed. *Sexism and Youth.* Bowker, 1974.

Gesell, Arnold and Frances Ilg. *Child Development: An Introduction to the Study of Human Growth.* Harper, 1949.

Gesell, Arnold and others. *The First Five Years of Life: A Guide to the Study of the Preschool Child.* Harper, 1940.

Ginott, Haim. *Between Parent and Child.* Macmillan, 1965.

Glazer, Susan Mandel. *Getting Ready to Read: Creating Readers from Birth to Six.* Prentice-Hall, 1980.

Gordon, Ira. *Baby Learning Through Baby Play: A Parent Guide for the First Two Years.* St. Martin's, 1970.

Gordon, Ira, Barry Guinagh, and Emile Jester. *Child Learning Through Child Play: Learning Activities for Two and Three-Year-Olds.* St. Martin's, 1978.

Haviland, Virginia, ed. *Children and Literature: Views and Reviews.* Scott, Foresman, 1973.

Haviland, Virginia. *Children's Literature: A Guide to Reference Sources.* Library of Congress, 1966.

Hazard, Paul. *Books, Children, and Men.* trans. by Marguerite Mitchell, fourth edition. Horn Book, 1960.

Hearne, Betsy and Marilyn Kaye, eds. *Celebrating Children's Books.* Lothrop, Lee & Shepard, 1981.

Hoffman, Miriam and Eva Samuels, eds. *Authors and Illustrators of Children's Books: Writings on Their Lives and Works.* Bowker, 1972.

Hopkins, Lee Bennett. *Books Are By People.* Citation, 1969.

———*More Books By More People.* Citation, 1974.

Huck, Charlotte and Doris Young Kuhn. *Children's Literature in the Elementary School,* third edition. Holt, 1976.

Hunter, Mollie. *Talent Is Not Enough.* Harper, 1976.

Jacobs, Leland B., ed. *Using Literature with Young Children.* Teacher's College Press, 1965.

Johnson, Edna, Evelyn Sickels, and Frances Clarke Sayers. *Anthology of Children's Literature,* fourth edition. Houghton Mifflin, 1970.

Karl, Jean. *From Childhood to Childhood: Children's Books and Their Creators.* Day, 1970.

Kellogg, Rhonda and Scott O'Dell. *The Psychology of Children's Art.* Random House, 1967.

Klemin, Diana. *The Art of Art for Children's Books.* Potter, 1966.

———*The Illustrated Book: Its Art and Craft.* Potter, 1966.

Koch, Kenneth. *Wishes, Lies, and Dreams. Teaching Children to Write Poetry.* Random House, 1971.

Kohl, Herbert. *Reading: How To.* Dutton, 1972.

Lanes, Selma G. *Down the Rabbit Hole: Adventures and Misadventures in the Realm of Children's Literature.* Atheneum, 1971.

Larrick, Nancy. *A Parent's Guide to Children's Reading,* fourth edition. Doubleday, 1975.

———*A Teacher's Guide to Children's Books.* Merrill, 1960.

———ed. *Somebody Turned on the Tap in These Kids.* Delacorte, 1971.

Marzollo, Jean and Janice Lloyd. *Learning Through Play.* Harper, 1972.

Marzollo, Jean. *Supertot: Creative Learning Activities for Children One to Three and Sympathetic Advice to Their Parents.* Harper, 1979.

Meeker, Alice M. *Enjoying Literature With Children.* Odyssey, 1969.

Meigs, Cornelia, Anne Eaton, Elizabeth Nesbitt, and Ruth Hill Viguers. *A Critical History of Children's Literature.* Macmillan, 1969.

Piaget, Jean and Barbel Inhelder. *The Psychology of the Child.* trans. from the French by Helen Weaver. Basic, 1969.

Pitz, Henry C. *Illustrating Children's Books: History, Technique, Production.* Watson-Guptil, 1963.

Princeton Center for Infancy, Frank Caplan, ed. *The Parenting Advisor.* Doubleday, Anchor, 1976.

Rudman, Marsha Kabakow. *Children's Literature: An Issues Approach.* Heath, 1976.

Smith, Lillian. *The Unreluctant Years.* ALA, 1953, reissued by Viking, 1967.

Sparling, Joseph and Isabelle Lewis. *Learning Games for the First Three Years: A Guide to Parent-Child Play.* Walker, 1978.

Sprung, Barbara. *Non-Sexist Education for Young Children.* Citation, 1975.

———ed. *Perspectives on Non-Sexist Early Childhood Education.* Teacher's College Press, 1978.

Szasz, Susanne. *The Body Language of Children.* Norton, 1978.

Townsend, John Rowe. *A Sense of Story.* Longmans, 1971.

Wyndham, Lee. *Writing for Children and Teen-agers.* Writer's Digest, 1968.

Yolen, Jane. *Writing Books for Children.* The Writer, Inc., 1973.

PUBLISHERS' DIRECTORY

Addison-Wesley Publishing Co., Inc.
Jacob Way
Reading, Massachusetts 01867

Atheneum Publishers
597 Fifth Avenue
New York, New York 10017

Bantam Books
666 Fifth Avenue
New York, New York 10019

Beacon Press
25 Beacon Street
Boston, Massachusetts 02108

R.R. Bowker and Co.
1180 Avenue of the Americas
New York, New York 10036

Bradbury Press, Inc.
2 Overhill Road
Scarsdale, New York 10583

Childrens Press
1224 West Van Buren Street
Chicago, Illinois 60607

Coward, McCann & Geoghegan, Inc.
200 Madison Avenue
New York, New York 10016

Crowell Junior Books
10 East 53 Street
New York, New York 10022

Crown Publishers, Inc.
One Park Avenue
New York, New York 10016

Delacorte Press
1 Dag Hammarskjold Plaza
245 East 47 Street
New York, New York 10017

Dell Publishing Co., Inc.
1 Dag Hammarskjold Plaza
245 East 47 Street
New York, New York 10017

Dial Press
1 Dag Hammarskjold Plaza
245 East 47 Street
New York, New York 10017

Dodd, Mead & Co., Inc.
79 Madison Avenue
New York, New York 10016

Doubleday & Co. Inc.
245 Park Avenue
New York, New York 10017

E.P. Dutton
2 Park Avenue
New York, New York 10016

Farrar, Straus & Giroux, Inc.
19 Union Square West
New York, New York 10003

The Feminist Press
SUNY at Old Westbury
Box 334
Old Westbury, New York 11568

Four Winds Press
50 West 44 Street
New York, New York 10036

The Free Press (Division of Macmillan)
866 Third Avenue
New York, New York 10022

Golden Press
850 Third Avenue
New York, New York 10022

Green Tiger Press
7458 La Jolla Blvd.
La Jolla, California 92038

Greenwillow Books
105 Madison Avenue
New York, New York 10016

Grosset & Dunlap, Inc.
51 Madison Avenue
New York, New York 10010

Harcourt Brace Jovanovich, Inc.
757 Third Avenue
New York, New York 10017

Harper & Row, Publishers, Inc.
10 East 53 Street
New York, New York 10022

Harvey House Publishers
20 Waterside Plaza
New York, New York 10010

Hastings House Publishers, Inc.
10 East 40 Street
New York, New York 10016

Holiday House, Inc.
18 East 53 Street
New York, New York 10022

Holt, Rinehart & Winston
383 Madison Avenue
New York, New York 10017

The Horn Book, Inc.
Park Square Building
31 St. James Avenue
Boston, Massachusetts 02116

Houghton Mifflin Co.
2 Park Street
Boston, Massachusetts 02108

Houghton Mifflin/Clarion Books
52 Vanderbilt Avenue
New York, New York 10017

Human Sciences Press, Inc.
72 Fifth Avenue
New York, New York 10011

Alfred A. Knopf, Inc.
201 East 50 Street
New York, New York 10022

Lippincott Junior Books
10 East 53 Street
New York, New York 10022

Little, Brown & Co.
34 Beacon Street
Boston, Massachusetts 02106

Lollipop Power
Box 1171
Chapel Hill, North Carolina 27514

Lothrop, Lee & Shepard Books
105 Madison Avenue
New York, New York 10016

Macmillan Publishing Co., Inc.
866 Third Avenue
New York, New York 10022

McGraw-Hill Book Co.
1221 Avenue of the Americas
New York, New York 10020

David McKay Co., Inc.
2 Park Avenue
New York, New York 10016

Charles E. Merrill Publishing Co.
(Bell & Howell Co.)
1300 Alum Creek Drive
Columbus, Ohio 43216

Methuen, Inc.
733 Third Avenue
New York, New York 10017

William Morrow & Co., Inc.
105 Madison Avenue
New York, New York 10016

Oxford University Press, Inc.
200 Madison Avenue
New York, New York 10016

Pantheon Books, Inc.
201 East 50 Street
New York, New York 10022

Parents Magazine Press
52 Vanderbilt Avenue
New York, New York 10017

Penguin Books
625 Madison Avenue
New York, New York 10022

Philomel Books
200 Madison Avenue
New York, New York 10016

Platt & Munk
(Division of Grosset & Dunlap)
51 Madison Avenue
New York, New York 10010

Clarkson N. Potter, Inc.
One Park Avenue
New York, New York 10016

Prentice-Hall, Inc.
Englewood Cliffs, New Jersey 07632

Price/Stern/Sloan Publishers, Inc.
410 N. La Cienega Blvd.
Los Angeles, California 90048

G.P. Putnam's Sons
200 Madison Avenue
New York, New York 10016

Random House, Inc.
201 East 50 Street
New York, New York 10022

St. Martin's Press
175 Fifth Avenue
New York, New York 10010

Scholastic Books
50 West 44 Street
New York, New York 10036

Scott, Foresman & Co.
1900 East Lake Avenue
Glenview, Illinois 60025

Charles Scribner's Sons
597 Fifth Avenue
New York, New York 10017

The Seabury Press, Inc.
815 Second Avenue
New York, New York 10017

Simon & Schuster, Inc.
1230 Avenue of the Americas
New York, New York 10022

The Viking Press
625 Madison Avenue
New York, New York 10022

Walker & Co.
720 Fifth Avenue
New York, New York 10019

Frederick Warne & Co., Inc.
2 Park Avenue
New York, New York 10016

Franklin Watts, Inc.
730 Fifth Avenue
New York, New York 10019

John Weatherhill, Inc.
149 Madison Avenue
New York, New York 10016

Albert Whitman & Co.
560 West Lake Street
Chicago, Illinois 60606

Windmill Books, Inc.
(Division of Simon & Schuster)
1230 Avenue of the Americas
New York, New York 10020

World Publishing Co.
(Division of William Collins Publishers Inc.)
2080 West 117 Street
Cleveland, Ohio 44111

ABOUT THE AUTHOR

After completing a master's degree in English at The State University of New York at Binghamton, Mary Jane Mangini Rossi combined her love for both children and books by becoming immersed in the world of children's literature. She teaches children's literature at Somerset County College in North Branch, New Jersey, and reviews children's books for various publications. Mary Jane is also an early childhood educator and has taught English at Trenton State College in New Jersey. Eager to share her love for children's books, she hatched The Book Stork, a mail-order children's book selection and consultation service that is flying good books to children in the U.S. and abroad. Mary Jane has spoken about children's literature on both T.V. and radio and conducts workshops for parents and children at schools and infant centers. Mary Jane shares a house in Princeton, New Jersey, with her husband, a few plants, and hundreds of children's books.